Live Like It Matters

And

Love Like Crazy

Live Like It Matters

And

Love Like Crazy

By

Beth Ann Stockton

Surprise, Arizona

Live Like It Matters

And

Love Like Crazy

Beth Ann Stockton

Live Like It Matters and Love Like Crazy.

All rights reserved. No part of this book may be reproduced or transmitted in any form or by any means, electronic or mechanical, including photocopying, recording or by any information storage and retrieval system, without written permission from the author, except for the inclusion of brief quotations in a review.

Copyright © 2016 by Beth Ann Stockton

First Edition, 2016

Front & Back Cover by Doug Tolf.

Published in the United States of America

I dedicate this book to my three children, Liam, Luke and Madeline. May you always be true to yourself and be kind to others. Live your life with full integrity and full of love and laughter. All three of you have inspired me to be a better mother and person. I also want to say thank you to my husband, Chris, for your truth and honestly in writing this book, also your friendship, love and support. Without you, this book would not be possible.

Also, thank you to my family and friends who are amazing and who I love so much.

Thank you all,

Beth Ann Stockton

We all want what is best for ourselves in life; but staying committed and strong every day, can be hard. Encouragement and knowing we are not alone in finding this, helps us in our journey to find peace, love and some great friendships along the way.

Live Like It Matters
And
Love Like Crazy

Chapter 1
 Introduction

Chapter 2
I vow to LIVE my life with purpose and truth.

Chapter 3
I vow to not merely LIVE for myself but to LIVE for others.

Chapter 4
I vow to LIVE with honesty and be loyal in everything I do.

Chapter 5
I vow to LIVE with integrity and conviction.

Chapter 6
I vow to LIVE my life to the fullest and have meaning to my words and truth to my actions.

Live Like It Matters And Love Like Crazy

Chapter 7
I vow to LIVE my life with strength and be crazy courageous every day I am alive.

Chapter 8
I vow to let LOVE lead me and leave the hate behind.

Chapter 9
I vow to LOVE above evil and judgment.

Chapter 10
I vow to LOVE when it just does not seem possible.

Chapter 11
I vow to LOVE my family, my friends, and my enemies.

Chapter 12
I vow to LOVE beyond measure because life is a treasure.

My name is Beth Ann Stockton. I am a mother of three children and have been married to my best friend for over 15 years. I have been writing for a long time. I started writing when I was around 15 years old. Writing just made me feel better. I knew at a young age that my life would be different. Going through life with all its ups and downs, you have to find balance and you have to know that you are here for a reason and that your life matters. I know, for me, I needed that because I wanted to know what my purpose on this earth was. My faith in God and my foundation for my life is very important to me. Early in my life I started to realize that, I want to make people smile and know that even on a hard day, there is hope and that we are all in this wonderful thing called life together.

Thank you to the people who inspired me and believed in me during the writing of this book.

Chris, My Husband

Betty, My Mother

John, My Father

Jennifer, My Twin Sister

Chapter one

Live Like It Matters

And

Love Like Crazy

Live Like It Matters And Love Like Crazy! If you ask yourself this enough, you will start to think am I living this way, or is this really too hard to do with all that I have been through? Life brings us to unexpected places sometimes. Situations we never thought would come our way actually do. Maybe you are not sure about your life or where it is going.

Let me ease your mind. Most of us don't know where our lives are going because if we did, than that would mean we have 100% control of our lives and that's just not true.

I started to write this book on this very thought.

Live Like It Matters and Love Like Crazy. My life has had its shares of heart ache and pain. My life has had its challenges and frustrations. I have also had many positive and wonderful experiences that led me to write *Live Like it Matters and Love Like Crazy*. I was able to get out all those feeling and it became my outlet for the things I have been through. As I would write, I started to really ask myself this very question, of am I living my life like it mattered and do I love like crazy?

My answer was NO. So the more I wrote the more I would catch myself asking myself the questions Do I live my life like it matters? Do I love like crazy? When life gets hard, what am I doing in those hard times? Do I love like crazy even when I don't want to love or don't know how to love?

We all have read self-help books and books that might have helped us through a hard time and there are some amazing books that have been written. The one book that has held its truth and has been my salvation through life is the Bible.

I did not write this book because I have all the answers or that because my life is easy. I wrote it because I want to make a difference in our world and it involves ALL of us. We all need to be a part of this world and bring peace back, bring love back and bring kindness back. It starts with you and me. We need to take the focus off ourselves and remember we are all just trying to wake up and breathe and get through the day in one piece.

Take this challenge with me and read this book. Find out about yourself and where you want your life to go.

Why are you here? What is it about you and the things that have shaped your life mean? Make a VOW to change the way you think about your life and the lives of others people too.

LIVE LIKE IT MATTERS

AND

LOVE LIKE CRAZY?

Live Like It Matters And Love Like Crazy! What does that mean? What kind of life struggles have you gone through that would hinder you from living your life to the fullest? What experiences have you been through in your life that would change the way you look at other people's lives?

Take a moment and write a few of your thoughts down in the space below.

Have you asked yourself "**WHY** does my life matter?"

WHO does it matter to?

How can you love like crazy when sometimes you wonder how do I even love myself?

This book is about making a change even if you don't know how. This book is about you and standing up for what is important to you.

I knew at a young age that my life was different. I have a twin sister named Jennifer and her life has forever changed me. We were born one minute apart. She was born with a brain injury from lack of oxygen getting to her brain. She is brain damaged and she is blind. I knew there was a reason for her in my life. As I grew older I knew something inside of me was changing and my faith became stronger and my purpose on this earth became vital to who I wanted to be. My understanding for life and that no one is perfect was becoming real.

I learned that bad things can happen to good people and that you have to work through the situation and never give up. See, I don't want us to just live our life's day in and day out, but to have meaning and purpose in it.

That is why I wrote this Declaration. This is a VOW and a decision to LIVE your life for more than what is just in front of you.

Writing *Live Like It Matters and Love Like Crazy* does not mean I am an expert at it. I started to write this book because I felt like I needed to change something in my own life. I don't always live like it matters and I don't always love like crazy. I didn't write this book to preach to you and tell you how to live your life. I wrote this because when you think about it, does your life matter or do you love like crazy? It makes you think about your day, and it makes you think about the people that you interact with. It also makes you think about why you are here. We all have rough days. We all go through terrible situations and have tragedy in our lives. There might be somebody out there that you will not be able to love like crazy and it will be a challenge every day. There might be days that you wake up and you don't care to live like it matters you just want to hide under the covers. But once your life is over, there's no coming back to live like it matters; there's no coming back to make a change. There's no coming back to love somebody like crazy so the time is **NOW!**

The time is **NOW** to be crazy about loving and the time is **NOW** to live like it matters because once your life is over, it is what people will remember about you when you are gone that mattered.

Don't be afraid to fall and don't be afraid to fail. It will happen, whether you try or not, that's how you learn and that's how you grow as a person. You get back up.

Maybe you feel like you don't belong. Maybe you feel like you are not normal, but I think we all feel like that sometimes. It's ok to feel that way. What is normal anyway?

As I was writing this, I heard one of my favorite songs by Matthew West. The name of the song is called "Do Something" and it affected me so much. The words in the song are very real and deep. The point to the song is why are we here? Let's not just sit around and wait for someone else to change something. God created us for a purpose and we need to open our eyes and our hearts and love people and give back.

Live your life every day and have meaning to it. I know that for me the changing point was when I was 19 years old and my family fell apart. I thought to myself where do I belong now?

My parents were married for 25 years and suddenly they got a divorce and it was the saddest day ever so I thought. In my mind, their marriage was perfect. I never saw them fight. I didn't understand what was to come and what it was supposed to mean and what it was supposed to show me.

My parents were amazing parents. They gave me love and support. They were involved in my life. Both my parents worked and as I got older my dad traveled for his job. They were there for me in all my school and life activities. I feel so blessed to have them as parents. But when you are young you don't think about bad things happening to you. I use to think having a sister with disabilities was our challenge in our home, that nothing else would go wrong. I never thought it would be my parents getting the divorce.

During my parent's marriage they had their struggles and challenges, just like we all go through. My parents raised three children. Mark, my brother is 5 years older than me. Then there is my twin sister Jennifer and myself. Having a child with disabilities is emotionally and physically challenging. My parents went through so much for Jennifer. They had to see so many different doctors and just the thoughts of how do we do this? How do we raise a mentally and physically handicapped daughter? My mom wanted everything for my sister so she would try anything to improve her health and her growth. Both my parents worked to provide a great life for us. Underneath that life, though, were the struggles and some of the pain that we never really dealt with. No parent wants to show their child that they are hurting. I know that I have had times that I needed to be strong for my kids and it is not always easy.

My parents wanted to protect me from any pain or any struggles. But in reality, it hurt me because as I grew up I started to see the world through different eyes and the picture of this was dark on some days and sad. I think because my sister was not perfect that everything else in my life and within my family had to be perfect. The emptiness that my parent's felt was hidden and replaced with being busy and working, but never fully filling that void.

I rarely saw my parents fight. Sometimes things were pushed under the rug and never dealt with.

So when it was time for me to be on my own, and in my own relationships I could not handle certain things. I had never learned how to fight right or see conflicts and resolve them. Anger is real and it is not a bad thing. It is how you handle your anger. Feelings are real because they belong to that person. I had to find myself and my voice. I had to see things for what they really were and what was right in front of me and not think that it will work itself out or just go away. Feelings and problems need to be dealt with.

The attention had to be divided between all of us. As a mother of three, I totally understand how hard that must have been for my parents, especially with a handicap daughter. It is important to give your child that attention, spend time with them. Time is a blessing and you don't get it back.

So put down the dishes and spend time with your children. Listen to them because their feelings are important.

Sometimes it is easy to get busy in life and forget to enjoy life and the people in your life.
As we all want that attention in life from our parents we want to be told that they are proud of us.

My parents were very proud of me no matter what I did but the divorce definitely changed my life.

I was angry and sad that our family was not together. I felt alone in my life. I know that their marriage was not my fault, but I did not understand why they could not work it out. I had to let go of those feeling and move on in my life. I had to forgive them and love them for the people they are, and not the marriage they once had. That was hard because as a young adult I only could relate to them as my parents and not as individual people.

There comes a point when you ask yourself, why am I here? What does my life mean? Are you going to be angry and bitter? Being angry and bitter will just make you feel alone and will empty your soul. Life is very sad and lonely when you fill it with anger and bitterness and an unforgiving heart.

Some of you out there might be saying that this is too hard and what is the point. That is why I wrote this for myself. I needed a reason for my life to have meaning and a reason to be happy. I needed a way to let myself know that I will fall, but I will get back up and that I can bend and won't break. That is why I'm writing this book. Life can be hard. No one said it would be easy. Keep your faith. Keep believing in yourself. Never give up.

Chapter two

I Vow To LIVE My Life

With

Purpose and Truth

What is your purpose in this life?

     The definition for the word purpose is the feeling of being determined to do or achieve something. What is your purpose? Is it a feeling inside you that no matter what happens, you will not give up? Is your purpose for your life an idea of what you want to achieve. We all have a purpose in our lives.

Let your purpose be bigger than you are, let your purpose drive you and take you into life with meaning and passion.

Genesis 1: 26-27 NIV

Then God said, "Let us make mankind in our image, in our likeness, so that they may rule over the fish in the sea and the birds in the sky, over the livestock and all the wild animals, and over all the creatures that move along the ground." So God created mankind in his own image, in the image of God he created them; male and female he created them.

You were made in his image so you do have purpose.

Who am I?

What am I meant to do here on this earth?

What am I going to do with my life?

Think about those questions.

Write down some notes on your journey. The only person who can answer these questions is you, and only you know the truth and can see your purpose.

Answer the questions I am asking you.

Who am I really?

What am I meant to do on this earth?

What am I going to do with my life?

Write down your thoughts in the space below

Every person is a unique being. There is only one of you in this world. **ONLY ONE YOU!!!!!!!!!!**

You have your own gifts and talents and ideas that no one else has.

Jeremiah 29:11NIV

" For I know the plans I have for you," declares the Lord, "plans to prosper you and not to harm you, plans to give you hope and a future.

Unless you surrender to Jesus, you will not know his will for your life.

What is TRUTH?

Truth is the real facts about something. That is the Webster's definition of truth.

But TRUTH exposes the real you. Truth is being vulnerable and letting people see the real you. Wise men seek truth and the truth is just the truth and nothing else. It sets you free.

Ephesians 6:14-18

So stand strong, with the belt of truth tied around your waist and the protection of right living on your chest. On your feet wear the Good News of peace to help you stand strong. And also use the shield of faith with which you can stop all the burning arrows of the Evil One. Accept Gods salvation as your helmet, and take the sword of the spirit, which is the word of God. Pray in the spirit all the times with all kinds of prayers, asking for everything you need. To do this you must always be ready and never give up. Always pray for all God's people.

This scripture is so very important in this world today. We live in a world that if you are not protected you will get hurt. If you were to go into war you would make sure you have your full armor on from head to toe so you are protected. We live in a world that is in a war every day. Waking up for some of us is a war. Maybe getting to work on time or getting the kids to school. Maybe your marriage is in a war and you are striving every day to make it work?

What are your trials?

Write your thoughts on what your war is today.

What are you going through?

Maybe you have trials with your family. The ideas you have about your family and the way you thought it should be is not the way it is in reality.

The world is filled with so many people, that we are bound to not always agree with someone. Being at war with someone or even ourselves is hard. It breaks relationships and it destroys lives. You have to know who you are and what you want for your life. Have that purpose and truth to live by every day. I know for me that having a twin sister that is mentally and physically handicapped made me see things in a way that challenged me. It made me stronger and made me want to keep going and never stop learning and growing and giving. It also opened my eyes to the true meaning of life and it is not fancy cars or having lots of money. It's not about looking perfect, or pretending to be something I am not.

Knowing I have purpose and knowing the truth about my life and how to find that truth was very important to me.

As I said earlier my sister and I are twins. I use to think that it would be awesome to have a sister to talk to about boys and clothes and all the things of life. I thought how fun it would be to look the same and all that comes with being a twin. But my case is a little different.

My sister and I were born on May 7, 1977. A few weeks before we were born, my mom went into early labor. The doctors put my mom on bed rest and told her she needed to relax and prevent her labor because our lungs were not yet fully developed. A few weeks later, at 34 weeks, we were born. As the doctors prepared for a C-section, my mom had no idea that her life was about to change. My mother was highly medicated and was not awake during the procedure. When my mother woke up from the anesthesia, she wanted to know how her babies were.

Technology over 35 years ago was not the same as it is today. There was no way of knowing what my parents were about to see. My sister had the umbilical cord around her neck 7 times. It was cutting off the circulation and oxygen to her brain. When we were born my mom had no idea of the seriousness of my sister and what had happened. She had to find hope within herself because there was no hope given to her. After Jennifer and I were born, Jennifer was in the hospital for an additional 6 weeks.

She was in an incubator because her lungs were not fully developed and she had brain damage. I was only 4 pounds but my lungs were stronger so my mom was able to bring me home after about a week.

As a mother of three, I cannot imagine what my mom went through. Becoming a mom changes you no matter how you look at it, but having twins and one with medical issues truly changes your life. No mother wants to go through the feeling of one of her children having difficulties or challenges in life. Not having the resources and the support, like they have available today, made her feel alone and lost.

When things calmed down and my mom was able to understand what had happened. The doctor said you have two daughters. One who is healthy and will live a normal life and your other daughter who is severely brain damaged and blind and will not be able to do much. The doctor told my mom that Jennifer would be a vegetable and would most likely not live past 7 years-old.

You don't ever tell a mother that your child will be nothing.

I think from that day on my mother had more courage in her and more fire to prove everyone wrong. I think that fight my mother had is what makes me a strong woman today. I know my mom wanted the best for her two daughters and was going to take nothing less than that. Both my parents had a drive and a fight that was inside them and it taught me to never give up on life.

So from a young age I knew I had no choice but to live my life like it matters and to love like crazy. My twin sister shaped my entire life and my family's lives. My twin sister was a gift. I know you might say, "How is having a sister with brain damage and who is blind, a blessing?" I can tell you every day how much I wish she was normal and how I want her to see me, but the truth is that is not going to happen, and the sooner I accepted it the better I felt. I have that guilt of why her and not me. Why am I here today living out a normal life and not her. She is my gift because she reminds me that there is no normal, there is no perfect. There is just you and me and the life we have been given. She is my gift of peace and calmness. She brings joy and love and laughter with no expectations. She loves with no reservation. Growing up with Jennifer I knew we shared a special bond that no one else shared.

The emotional and physical journey in being a part of someone's life with mental and physical disabilities was draining at times. Someone always had to be caring for her and helping her. Jennifer would crawl all over the house if she was not in her wheelchair. She needed help with everything. Jennifer needed help feeding herself every day with every meal. She needed help cleaning up after each meal. Someone had to sit with her to make sure she was eating ok. It was like having a baby in the house and she was not a baby anymore. My mother played the piano almost every day when we were young. She would sing and play and Jennifer would listen to my mom. I know it was something Jennifer loved. It calmed her down. My sister would crawl up to the piano and play Twinkle Twinkle Little Star. Jennifer learned how to play by listening to my mom play. When we were little my sister was much smaller than me and she moved her head around because she is blind.

People use to come up to my mom and say what cute babies and look at both of us and say what is wrong with her. They were referring to my sister. My mom got so tired of hearing this. One day she finally said "I am doing an experiment and feeding one and not the other." People looked at her like she was crazy. The truth is people were rude and insensitive. Our home was always busy and Jennifer needed continuous care.

Jennifer had to have physical therapy for her legs to help her get strong and keep the blood flow going since she could not walk. I was always there to help her in the bathroom or help get her dressed. I always wanted to help her. Jennifer loves playing ball and listening to movies. The older we got the harder it got. When we were teenagers and I was doing things on my own, Jennifer was still at home or in need of care all the time. My parents had caregivers to help out when they had to work. My sister went to the a special program during the day, but it was every night that someone had to be there to bathe her, feed her and make sure she got her medicine and put her to bed. I remember sharing a room and talking to her at night. Her medicine was for her seizures. As she got older too she learned how to start to do some of these things on her own with a little bit of help.

There were times she would make me laugh so hard. There were times that I would just sit at the kitchen table saying goofy things to make her laugh. I needed it as much as she did. My older brother Mark was there and he would talk to her and hang out too. Jennifer was the only one I had. My twin sister's words were unclear to a lot of people. I understood them and so did my brother and parents, but not many people do. The brain damage affected her brain and how she hears words and processes them.

Also the fact that she is blind made it harder for her to understand what was going on around her. Going places was not always easy. My parents had to always think of situations first and what about Jenny. My sister learned a lot as she got older. With the help of my parents, my brother and I, she learned so much. We also had caretakers that came in and taught Jennifer how to do things for herself. Jennifer became more independent. Jennifer learned how to do some little things for herself. She learned how to walk with a walker to the bathroom. She always needed assistance but the fact that she was doing things on her own was huge. Jennifer learned how to swim, which was a big deal for her and the rest of the family. We could interact with her in the pool and it was a lot of fun. This also became her exercise. She needed assistants in and out of the pool, but she loved swimming. This was a huge for Jennifer because it made her smile and made her feel happy. Jennifer loves to have fun and she loves going to the movies even though she is blind. She listens to the movies.

    I know that having children can change a person and can change a marriage. I know Jennifer's everyday life put a strain on my parents as individuals and in their marriage. It took a toll on them and I think in the beginning they wanted everything to be normal and they tried so hard to make it that way, but there was nothing normal about our family.

My mom tried so hard to get the best for Jennifer and she put everything she had into her. I admire her for that. The marriage became more about Jennifer and less about them. The talking became less and the business of life took over. I think sometimes we hide behind our pain so we don't face it. We all do it sometime or another in our life.

I am not saying my parents did not work hard in their marriage but what I am saying is life brings us to places we might not have ever dreamed good or bad and it's what we do with our circumstances and how we learn to grow through them not against them. I know my parents' marriage is not based off Jennifer's life for sure. There were other things that caused them to divorce. I think for me the knowing that she will never be normal was something I woke up to everyday. Knowing someone had to help her no matter what we were feeling, she needed us. In a way we needed her too. She kept me grounded and helped me realize life. What's important and what is not. As we grew older, into adults Jennifer stood out a lot more than when she was younger.

I know some people have a hard time seeing people like Jennifer because they don't know what to say or how to act, but Jennifer is no different than anyone else in the world. See, we all have some disability one way or another. Jennifer's are just more out in the open than others.

Inside each of us, there is need for improvement or something we need to work on. Maybe you are more of a selfish person or a materialist person. Maybe you are shy and introverted.

Maybe you talk too much or not enough. See Jennifer was born the way she is and so were you. The only difference is you can change somethings about yourself and learn from seeing people from the inside out instead of from the outside in. No one is perfect and Jennifer showed me that. It's what you do with what you have that makes your life better.

Having Jennifer in my life changed everything. I mean everything. I became very sensitive to a lot of things a normal little girl would not normally be sensitive to.

I looked at people differently. I was aware of people's differences. I was sensitive to the needs of others. I tried to see people from the inside out instead of from the outside in. Knowing Jennifer changed my life and I saw her disabilities as just something you have to deal with and rise above. I would look at other people and think they might need that extra love or that understanding, because they might not get it from other people. My sister's life changed mine because nothing or no one looked normal and that was ok.

My sister would sing and laugh. She loved to talk and have people talk to her. She loved hugs and kisses. She loved listening to all the Disney movies. Her favorites are Snow White and Little Mermaid. She also love's Annie. Jennifer has a laugh that lights up the room. I shared a room with Jennifer and was always there for her.

I understood at a very young age that Jennifer had brain damage and that she would never be normal. It never changed my love for her, it only made it stronger.

When I was around 7 years old, my mother's father passed away from cancer and it was very upsetting of. When we were at the gathering after the funeral, my brother and sister and I were surrounded with our family. Everyone was upset and sad. I was very sad and when I get sad or start to cry my sister does too. I looked over at my sister and knew something was wrong. I knew right away that she was having a seizure. My parents did not believe me. They thought I was just so upset and so were they that they brushed it off. I was persistent and I did not give up. They finally believed me when they saw Jennifer's face and knew; yes she was having a seizure. They rushed her to the hospital and got her the medication she needed.

A year later, Jennifer had another seizure. We shared a room for most of our childhood. My parents were in their room and I was with my sister in our room and I felt like something was wrong with Jenny, so I went to my parent's room right away. She was having another seizure. My parents had to rush her off again to the hospital. I felt like I was there for a reason to be my sister's voice. The connection and the bond between Jennifer and I is so strong.

If your life has truth, then keep it close to you. If there is truth in your friendships, family and in yourself you will cherish it. If your life has purpose, that purpose will keep you strong.

When I was 13 years old I had my first pair of glasses. I wanted my sister to see so badly. I wanted her to see me and smile at me and have that connection. I went up to my sister and put the glasses on her and prayed over her. I wanted to know if God would perform a miracle and make her see with my glasses. When I was done praying for her, I took the glasses off and asked my sister, "Jennifer, can you see me?" She just laughed and went on as if nothing had happened.

That was the day I realized that my sister wasn't going to be any different. She wasn't going to see. She wasn't going to be healed from the brain damage. She was born that way and there was nothing I or anyone else could do to change that. It became a reality for me.

That was hard at that age because I really wanted my sister to be normal. She has made me a better person by allowing me to see life through her eyes. She has made me a better person because in this world we can get caught up in all the things that don't matter and forget what does matter. The little things like a simple hug or telling someone you care. I want to always remember what is important in life.

I will always be her voice and share our story of how two sisters share a bond. I want to be her eyes and her voice so I can share with you that we are all created uniquely and are equal in God's eyes. I want to be a voice for her to share God's love and his will for our life.

When I was 15 my mom told me about a writing contest in the paper. She told me I should send in one of my poems. I loved to write poems, stories and songs. It was my way of expressing my feelings. So I sent in one of my poems and it was published in this book filled with lots of great poems written by other writers. The poem I submitted was called "**Jennifer's Smile** ".

It was one of the very first things I wrote. I had very deep and real emotions about my sister and I had lots of confusing thoughts about why she was the way she was. I carried a lot of guilt inside. I wondered why I am here, and why it was not me. Things happen for a reason and I am blessed to be here on this earth and I won't waste one minute of it. You don't expect life to go in the direction that it goes, but sometimes it does. Take it one day at a time and don't take a second for granted. You are here for a reason.

Jennifer's Smile

Seeing, what is it like?

Is it like laughing, crying

Not knowing the looks just sounds.

She is brain damaged, handicapped

The pain is like a hot steamed pot

Full of anger that spills, shatters to the ground

The pain I feel for my sister, shoot me, kill me

Do anything but not her.

Me, the victim

When I look at her I wonder, born one minute later

A minute too late, damaged like an earthquake

The brains in shreds

Overwhelming with sorrow

Where to turn next, seeing a smile that's all it took

I love my sister and accept her the way she is

So accept me as I do you

Accept the world with the problems too.

Find out what your Purpose is in life?

Find out what truth means to you. It might take a while so don't give up. Be patient with yourself and your life.

This is your life

And

It is a gift!

Chapter Three

I Vow To Not Merely LIVE My Life for Myself but to LIVE for Others

Proverbs 11:25

"A generous man will prosper; he who refreshes others will himself be refreshed."

There is a lot of truth to this. When you live a life only for yourself you will eventually start to feel alone. God never meant us to be alone or feel alone. He wants us to build relationships. When you build relationships you grow as a person. You can learn from each other.

I know that being real with people can be hard because you are putting yourself out there and being vulnerable. There are so many ways you can give to others. You have something about you that no one else has. You have talents and gifts that only you can share.

There are a lot of people hurting in the world. We just go about our own business never knowing how a simple smile or a conversation can change a person's life. Listening to someone might be the only thing they have to survive. Today we are so afraid to get close to anyone. We are all in our own bubble and afraid to reach out. We think if we get too close, then it gets too personal. Your privacy is important to you, and I understand that, but don't be afraid to share a smile or a helping hand.

When we are afraid to be real, it separates us from each other and if we keep thinking like this our world will be at war with everyone. Then we will be truly alone. When you can be open with others and know that you are not alone, then you can start to feel more peace about your life.

When you are thinking of "what can I do today for someone else" it takes the focus off ourselves and helps us reconnect with other people and connect with the world around us. We are important to God and he wants us to share our love, our pain, our grief and our happiness with others. When we share our life with others and our experiences, it shows we are real and that no one is perfect. It shows the world we are not alone and that we all go through some of the same things in life.

God came down in a form of a man and his name was Jesus. God wanted change to happen. He came to show that we need to love over the law and love over hypocrisy. God changed the world by having his son come down to show that love is real. Jesus redefined love. Jesus had one mission and that was to show us how to love God and one another.

He paid the price for our sins. He was here to show that we are all human. We all go through things in life and by opening ourselves up to one another we can grow as people.

In order for the people to know who this man was he needed followers who believed in him. The 12 disciples were not perfect men.

They had their doubts and their own sins. But together they shared Gods love and his message. They had one mission and that was to spread the love of Christ and to be a witness. Of course this came with a price. These men suffered great pain and loss. They knew they were leaving what was secure and safe. We, in America, have the right to follow any faith we would like. There are, of course, challenges with this. You may be judged for your faith. You may be looked at as an outcast but you are free to follow any faith or beliefs you wish to pursue.

Living life today can seem easy for some because when it comes to hard times and struggles it is easy to just walk away or ignore the problem. The problem will never go away for good. We need to be givers not takers. We need to be real and honest in life so our hearts can be filled with friendships and family and people who love us. If we don't then our heart will be filled with lies and doubt. Our souls will die to the lies and the hate.

Jesus wants us to love no matter what, no matter the cost. When we live for others it does something to us, it changes us. Live your life with meaning and give to others.

When you live for others it does something inside you. It changes you from the inside out. Makes you see that when you are there for others it opens your eyes to the real issues of every man and woman. It's ok to let people see your pain and that you are real.

Your pain might be someone else's saving grace or your grace might be the healing point in someone's life.

SMILE

Smiles are not all the same.

Some are BIG some are small.

Some don't look like smiles at all.

Everyone's smile is different in some way.

But they all have a story to say.

So don't be afraid to smile.

You just might make someone have a better day.

Seeing

Miracles

In

Life

Empower

Growing within yourself helps you find your way. It helps you love yourself and others. What would our world look like if everyone only looked out for themselves? In life, sometimes we think that if I just can get that next big thing then I will be happy.

It is only until the wow factor wears off and you are empty again and need something else to fill you up. It is just a sad cycle that never stops until you stop it. Until you see that not one thing will make you happy or complete. We must step outside of the four walls and see there is a whole world in front of us and people in it trying to survive just like us. We walk in our own shoes. We carry our own pain and feel our own joy but what are others going through. When we are walking down the street do we really know what's going on in someone's life. We can't see inside them, but we can reach out a hand and find out.

Are you reaching out to others and showing kindness and compassion. Or do we just judge them because of the way they look or sound. Or something they did or something they did not do.

I was in a fast-food drive through with my three kids one morning. The car in front of me had a Hello Kitty sticker on the back but the Hello Kitty was holding a gun. I started to judge the lady in the car. I said out loud "man that looks crazy "and my kids said, "What mom" and I said, "That lady has a sticker on her car". I continued to tell them it was a Hello Kitty holding a gun. I said something like that is crazy and weird to have that. I normally don't say things like that, but I did that day and my kids were following me in my judgment. As the car in front of me drove away and I pulled up to get my order, the lady at the window said that the woman in front of me paid for my order. I could not believe it. I was brought to tears. I felt so bad for judging her. I told my kids about it and I also told them that I was wrong. I said what if that women had a Hello Kitty sticker with a gun because she served in the military or something like that and just happens to really like Hello Kitty.

Or maybe she just likes guns. I learned a lesson that day and so did my kids. I showed them that I make mistakes and that we should not judge people. They also saw me right my wrong.

I have learned that loving people is not always easy and that the way I should treat people is important. I know that just because I treat people nice does not always mean I will get treated nice back. I wish it worked like that, but it doesn't. That is a hard lesson to learn. Not everyone will agree with you on your thoughts and opinions.

Matthew 7:12

So in everything, do to others what you would have them do to you, for this sums up the law and the prophets.

Life is filled with mysteries and if we try to solve them all we will never live life. We are always trying to find the meaning to things. Finding the meaning to life can be found in your friendships or in your family. You might even find life's meaning with a stranger. There does not have to be a reason to love people. There does not have to be an expectation to receive it back. I know that is hard. Trust me! That is where I find it hard. I give to others because I want to. My heart is filled with love and I want to share it, but not everyone is receiving of it. If we let go of reason and just trust, then maybe we can find a glimpse of hope.

Chapter Four

I Vow To LIVE With Honesty and to Be Loyal In Everything I Do

Honesty is the quality of being fair and truthful.

Do you feel like you are an honest person?

Do you feel like you live a life that is fair and true?

What does your character show each day?

Do you wear a mask?

Do you hide your true self behind a mask? Are you hiding from the real world? If you are living a lie it will slowly catch up to you, I promise. If you are just honest from the beginning, then there is nothing to hide from.

Loyalty is having or showing complete and constant support for someone or something.

When we live a life with honesty and we are loyal we stand for so much more. When we show loyalty and honesty, we are showing our family our friends, even our enemies that we care about the well-being of others and we want what is right for others. When you are a loyal friend, spouse or parent you are showing support to those who matter.

Also, like I said earlier, being honest and loyal means the mask is off. You will come across life's challenges and your situations where your faith will be put to the test. Who you want to be and, or who you strive to be will be influenced by certain people and their character qualities. You have to stay strong.

There will be situations in your life where your faith is tested and you will have to be honest. If you are a parent or maybe have a big influence on children then you need to know that your honesty and being loyal in everything you do will shape your kids for whom they will be. Staying honest and loyal in your marriage will just make it stronger. I have been married for over 16 years to my best friend Chris and I have been very honest in my marriage. I met Chris when I was 15 on a church retreat. There was something about him, and I wanted to get to know him more. We dated for 8 years before getting married. So we had a long time to get to know each other before we got married. It was not always easy. As young adults dating, we fought a lot.

The funny thing is we fought over some of the most ridiculous things that did not even matter. Those disagreements opened our eyes to the fact that we are two different people and that is okay; but if we want to love each other, then we have to grow with each other. We have learned a lot about each other and ourselves over the years. It has not always been easy. We have had some situations in our marriage where we both have had to make changes because we love each other. Being honest with each other has promoted opportunities for us to change and have a stronger relationship. I think that it is important in all relationships because how do you grow as people and how do we grow in our relationship if we are not honest?

We have learned over the years to always talk things out and if we disagree or get in a fight, we always work it out. With that being said, we have had tough times and times of uncertainty. We wanted to make things work but did not always know how. We are always learning from each other and I think that is the key to a healthy relationship. You have to have the willingness to learn and to grow with each other. Being open minded to learning and growing as a person makes the learning and loving easier.

Friendships are an important thing to have. Having friendships keeps us living. They keep us happy. In friendships you share your humor and your pain. You share your hopes and dreams for your life. Honest friends will be by your side through the toughest times in your life.

In a world of self-seekers and do what feels right, we need more real friendships that give instead of take. The root to a good friendship or marriage or any relationships is honesty and loyalty.

Have you heard the story of Job from the Bible?

This story tells a story of a man with great strength and loyalty to God.

Job 1:3

A man named Job lived in the land of Uz. He was an honest and innocent man; he honored God and stayed away from evil. Job had seven sons and three daughters. He owned seven thousand sheep, three thousand camels' five hundred teams of oxen, and five hundred female donkeys. He also had a large number of servants. He was the greatest man among all the people in the East.

Everything was going great for Job. He had it all, every blessing you could think of. He had a large family and lots of wealth. Job had tons of land and animals. But his blessed life bothered Satan.

The Lord said to Satan have you noticed my servant Job? No one else on earth is like him. He is an honest and innocent man honoring God and staying away from evil. But Satan answered the Lord, "Job honors God for a good reason. You have put a wall around him, his family, and everything he owns. You have blessed the things he has done. His flock and herd are so large they almost cover the land.

But reach out your hand and destroy everything he has, and he will curse you to your face. The Lord said to Satan, "Alright, then. Everything Job has is in your power, but you must not touch Job himself." Then Satan left the Lord's presence

Job 1:8-12

So Satan left the Lord's presence. He put sores on Job's body, from the top of his head to the soles of his feet. Job took a piece of broken pottery to scrape himself, and he sat in ashes in misery.

Job 2:7-10

Job's wife said to him, "Why are you trying to stay innocent? Curse God and die!" Job answered, "You are talking like a foolish woman. Should we take only the good things from God and not the trouble?" In spite of all this Job did not sin in what he said.

There are times in our lives that we will be tested and maybe even to the point where we want to give up and it is so easy to. We all get tired in life. The trials can defeat us and cause us to feel like there is no hope. That is just the trap that the devil wants us in. I know your life might be hard, but get up, get help, believe in yourself and believe in a loving God who created you to be something in this world. Your days on this earth are a mystery.

Live each day because it counts. Why is it when things are good we feel happy? But when things go wrong and they do, we find reasons to be angry and turn away from God or question Him on why me God? Instead we should not ask why, but what? What is God doing in my life? Job believed in God and that his faith would see him through his difficult trials.

Job had his land and his animals all taken from him. His family wiped away. He was left with nothings and no one. Yet he stayed faithful to God. He never cursed God during his trials. Today, we are up against so much. There is a pressure to have so many things and to keep up with the Joneses. Having the perfect marriage, or perfect kids or job. How do we handle the pressure?

Why do we have this pressure? What if you went to bed tonight and woke up and everything was gone. Maybe some of you are saying that happened to me. Life can pull you under like a strong wave in the ocean. Our faith is what keeps us strong. It is what kept Job strong and kept him believing when everything was taken away from him.

Job 1:21

He said "I was naked when I was born, and I will be naked when I die". He came into this world with nothing and if it was all taken from me then so be it. I leave with nothing.

What we have is not what we own. What we have does not define us. You can lose your things and still have your faith and your soul. You could look completely empty, but be completely full on the inside.

It is important to be loyal and true to ourselves and others. Today some people in this world look at honesty and loyalty as more of a waste of time compared to all of the other things they have going on in their lives.

Being honest and loyal means you are committed to yourself and to your family and friends. You will be there for them in the good times and bad times. What are we showing our kids if we are not honest? What can we leave behind? What can we instill in the future by being honest and loyal? What are we teaching our children?

Sometimes in life it seems easier to just quit and not keep trying or move on from relationship to relationship and not give it your all. Not one job is the most perfect job and not one relationship is the best and gives you all your needs. Life happens and how you live your life will determine how you live as a person and if you are content or not.

It is a choice and it is your choice. Choosing to live with honesty and loyalty will definitely help you live with more peace and in touch with the reality of life.

Write in the space below of how you can live with honesty and loyalty.

Chapter Five

I Vow To LIVE With Integrity and Conviction

Integrity is the quality of being honest and fair. The state of being complete or whole, taking full responsibility of your actions. But what is Integrity really? Integrity is your character even when no one is watching you. It's your morals and virtue. It's about being honest even when you know you might stand alone.

What does conviction mean?

Conviction is the feeling of being sure that what you believe or say is true.

What is conviction to you? Conviction is being strong and confident in who you are. It is having assurance in the choices you make.

What do you stand for today?

Trials will come our way in life, but it is how we handle those trials. It is how we handle those tough times that determine our character. Are you putting people's hearts and the feelings that they might feel over a situation? Or is the situation so much more important that we forget that there is a person behind the problem. So many times we get so caught up in the problems or the trials in our life that we forget that those problems are attached to people and their feelings. Feelings are neither right nor wrong it is just how a person is feeling. When you don't agree with your spouse or a friend, how are you treating them? Are you giving more importance to the situation and the problem than the person and their feeling? Situations will always be there until we are blue in the face, but our family and our friends will not. If we put a situation over a person's thoughts and emotions, what are we saying about that person?

What a person is feeling or going through is a moment of their life that needs attention in order to be able to move forward. If we focus more on the person and their heart instead of the situation, the outcome is much more positive. It does not mean that the situation is not important, or that it does not need to be dealt with. We need to care more about the person than the situation or the argument. People are not situations, they are people.

We live in a world filled with people who are not perfect. Family and friends are going to let you down and disappoint you. You can't give up. You have to keep trying.

When I was young I had a good childhood, played liked a normal kid, but in the back of my mind and in the front of my heart was my sister and all the thoughts of her and how to take care of her and give her love and attention. I would feel the guilt and sadness of not having a normal sister. I use to think that people might think that I am not smart because I have a twin sister with mental disabilities. As a child, you just don't understand fully what you are feeling. I mean I was in the same womb as my sister. I know that sounds crazy but I felt that way. I also felt like I have to be perfect because she is not.

I have to hold that standard. I know now that we were and are two different people but share a bond that will never be broken.

As I got older and became a teenager, I started to feel the trials of having a sister with disabilities. I saw things differently. I knew people looked at her differently and so I was looked at differently. I had thought, okay this is a tough thing to go through; but I knew it was a blessing also. I was not expecting more trials in my life. I was a kid, growing up in a home that seemed fine.

Growing up with a sister that was handicapped had its challenges. My parents worked and tried their best to do it all. They did what every parent tries to do and give all they can and raise the children right.

When you are young you don't have a good understanding of your integrity or what it means to have integrity. Sure you want to be fair and honest but to fully understanding yourself from the inside out **takes time and takes life**.

When you are young, you don't always understand your actions. There is a parent or an adult to help you get back up and learn through it.

Learning about who you are and what your character will be, only comes from you and your journey on this earth.

During my high school days, I felt sometimes misplaced -- like where do I belong? My sister went to the same high school with me and was there every day in her special class. I would visit her every day at lunch or between classes. I always felt this connection with her and knowing she was there meant so much to me. I think in some way I wanted her to be normal and walk around the school with her just like I did with my friends. It was very important to me. So when it came time to graduate I was told she could not go through the ceremony with me. I was upset and confused. My sister was in school every day and went through physical education classes and social interaction classes. She had teachers and lunch time just like all the rest of us. My mom spoke with the principal. She said Jennifer never missed a day of school and deserves to participate in the same ceremony just like everyone else. My parents were not afraid to ever speak up or be my sister's voice. My sister got to graduate and be part of the ceremony with me.

Walking with her knowing we were graduating together meant a lot to me and my family. It was a really great day and it was the beginning of my life as an adult.

My sister and I are so close to each other. Shortly after I graduated from high school, it was time for real life to begin. My parents made the decision for my sister to go into a group home with other adults her age that had similar disabilities. It was an emotional time for our family because my sister had always been in our home and I am sure it was very hard on my parents because it is always hard to let go of your kids.

My sister had a hard time at first but it really was good for her. I think that it was harder on us as a family to see her away from us. My parents took care of her for over 19 years and they were there for everything. My parents taught my sister to play the piano. My mom was there to teach my sister how to feed herself and dress herself. My sister learned how to swim and walk with a walker and so much more. My sister had amazing caregivers throughout her life that also helped her grow and helped my parents out. My parents were there for so much and now it was time to let go. I cannot express enough how hard that must have been for my parents and trusting other people to take care of her.

I know for me being a mom of three, I have my fears and doubts too. We always want the best for our kids.

A few short months later after my graduation and after my sister went into the group-home as I mentioned earlier, I found out some of the worst news ever. My parents were separating after 25 years of marriage. I cannot tell you how much that changed my life. I never thought this would happen.

I loved my parents so much and did not understand why. My heart broke that day. Going through my parent's divorce was hard. It was a long road to figure out my life and my relationship with my parents. I was angry for a long time because for me the divorce came out of nowhere, but not for my parents. I know now that the communication could have been better between them. Communication is hard in any relationship, but if it is not there then the relationship cannot grow. I learned more about real life after that day than I ever learned before because life became real to me and life's experiences became real to me.

I know that it is hard to make a marriage work. Not one person is the perfect spouse. It takes more than a lot of work. It takes Faith, Honesty and Forgiveness.

This time of my life became very lonely for me and it was a time that I guess I had to grow up and get to know myself instead of hiding under my parents.

I guess it was the first time in my life that I felt lost and had to start learning about this thing called life. I was not ready for this trial. I did not know how to handle the feelings that I was feeling.

I felt like it was my fault that they were divorcing. Growing up hearing all the talk about Jenny and the trials that they had to go through was hard. I was always thinking if there was something I could have done differently to save them or to work things out.

But it was not about me or Jennifer or my brother, it was about them not being honest and communicating the truth. It was easier to hide it and keep moving on.

It is kind of like a cut, if you keep putting a band aide on it and not let it breathe then it will never heal. Our hearts are open to love, but with that love come truth and sometimes pain. I wish my parents would have known that and worked it out, but they didn't and it is something that I have had to learn and grow from.

I know my parents had to grow within themselves during this hard time. I know my parents loved each other very much. It is hard to be vulnerable and put all of yourself out there. But it is worth it.

Chapter Six

I Vow to LIVE My Life to the Fullest and Have Meaning to My Words and Truth to My Actions

Living your life to the fullest can mean so many things for so many different people. We all go through life's challenges and pain, so find out what your life is missing. Find out how you can live your life to the fullest.

I know for me living my life means never giving up. It means giving to others as much as possible.

It means enjoy the little things about your life. When I found out about my parent's divorce my world stopped. Time really did stand still because I had no idea how to deal with the feeling and emotions that were in my head and on my heart.

My parent's divorce was finalized and I was confused. My mom moved out of our home and my dad remained at the house I grew up in. It was hard to be there without my mom. I did not know how to feel. I had to face what was in front of me and deal with it. I did not want to at all. I moved out of my home and it was the first time living on my own. I had lived in the same home my whole life. It was where I grew up and now I needed to leave all that. I started to feel like where is my life going now? I was getting ready to start college and should have been thinking about what I want to do with my life, but instead I was thinking about my parents and how confused I was.

How can I live my life to the fullest when my foundation was stripped from under me? I felt alone and unsure about life. I had the support of Chris (my husband now, but my boyfriend at that time), he knew me the best.

I would also talk to God and lean on him to get me through it. God knew my heart and the heaviness of it.

Finding myself in life and having meaning to my words and truth to my actions took a whole new meaning for me. I woke up that year and saw how life really was. People are real and life is real.

People are not perfect. People can hurt you. All things I believed were not true were true and I saw it first-hand. I was seeing the world for the first time through a clear perspective instead of a faded picture of what I thought life should be. I realized my parent's divorce was not about me or anything I did. I am thankful to my parents. They gave me life and gave my sister and brother life. They worked through and survived some crazy situations in their marriage that I cannot even begin to understand. They gave everything they had during their marriage and it just did not work. I love both my parents so much and have grown closer to them since their divorce. I also found out that you can forgive and love through the pain and grow as a person. I know life is not perfect because if it were, then my sister would be able to see and walk and live a normal life. She is a blessing that forever changed my life.

Love shapes us!

Kindness grows us!

Faith heals us!

My challenge to you is to not let circumstances keep you from living your life. Things are going to happen, you can't control them. Having meaning to your life means you live your life. It means you want to know what God has for you. It means give it all you got. It means work through the hurt and the pain. Don't waste your time on the wrongs of people, but on the good and build strong friendships and strong relationships with family and don't waste time on negative people. Even your enemies could use a smile or a helping hand. You never know what positive things can come from giving. If your life has purpose, what can you do to assure that your purpose has meaning?

Write in the space below what you feel your purpose in life should be.

Words speak loudly in this world.
Whether it is positive or negative people are listening and watching.

You must have truth to your actions.
We have all heard the saying, "If you love me prove it." Or, "If you love me so much, why are you not showing it." It is so very true. It's like a broken record. We can say I love you to someone a million times, but if our actions don't back them up then what is the point.

How can I show love?

You will still get mad about things and get frustrated about things and with people because that is natural, we are only human. Dealing with these feelings is important. Getting those feeling out is a vital key to getting through some of the deepest and darkest times in your life. You have to be real with people. But showing love, kindness and patience during this time is very important. It will not be easy but it is worth it.

My parents divorced changed my life forever. It showed me the reality of life. It showed me that people can make mistakes. It also showed me how to forgive. I did not want to forgive my parents. I was so sad that the divorce separated my family. I did not want to move on. I wanted two parents in one home. I wanted that family connection. What I wanted and needed was not a reality. I had to learn to move on. To forgive means to stop feeling anger towards someone who has done something to you. It means you stop blaming. It means you let it go. You don't have to agree with what happened. I was not ready to accept what had happened. I wanted everything to go back to the way it was. What I was feeling inside was normal, but eventually I had to accept what had happened. My expectations were unrealistic and I knew they were not going to get back together. I had to come to terms with their divorce.

The one thing that I've learned from this experience in life is if you don't have meaning to your words or truth to your action then you are left feeling empty.

Divorce is a confusing thing that can break families apart. But it is important to remember we are all human and we must survive on this earth day in and day out. Circumstances will change in life, but we must stay strong in our faith and know that God has a purpose for everything. Both my parents remarried and it was not something I was used to. But I must say I have a bigger family and that means more chances to give love and be a part of someone's life.

Have truth to your ACTIONS!!!

Chapter Seven

I Vow To LIVE My Life with Strength and To Be Crazy Courageous Every Day I Am Alive

Strength is the quality or state of being physically strong. It also means the ability to resist being moved or broken by force.

Courage *is the ability to do something that you know is difficult or dangerous. It also means a mental or moral strength to persevere, and withstand danger, fear or difficulty.*

What do these two words mean to you?

Who in your life has shown strength or courage?

Think about that for a minute. Who are you thinking about?

Below, make a list of people who have shaped your life and have changed it for the better. Also, make a list of people who have shown strength or courage.

There have been some significant people that have shown their strength and their courage. These people left a mark on our nation's history.

Helen Keller- she was deaf, blind and mute as a child. Many believed she would never accomplish anything. But yet she changed history and showed great strength to never give up on learning and the courage to share it with the world. We give up on the easiest things but she could not see or hear and she had a fire in her and a willingness to learn and to grow. Think about that. Her story of encouragement and the fierce fire to not give up is what can encourage us to never give up.

Mother Teresa - a leader of a group of nuns in India. She changed the way the world looked at helping the poor and the sick. Mother Teresa's faith was monumental and her soul was filled with the love of Christ. She helped give hope back to people in poverty. She was more than just a good Catholic; she was a self-sacrificing woman who loved God and people. She did not care who they were or where they came from. She wanted to spread God's love to everyone.

She spent many years in India serving the poor. She opened the first home for the dying in 1952. She wanted people to be able to die with dignity.

Mother Teresa had many amazing quotes; here are a few of my favorite.

"Not all of us can do great things. But we can do small things with great love." – Mother Teresa

"It is not how much we give, but how much love we put in the giving." Mother Teresa

In our society we give examples of amazing people who have given so much of their life to serving others. Mother Teresa is definitely one of those women. She was so pure in heart and so genuinely real and that is rare to find. Her quotes are so simple but true.

Rosa Parks- Rosa Louise McCauley Parks was her full name. Born February 4, 1913 and died October 24, 2005. She was a black woman who showed great strength and a lot of courage in a time that was so dangerous to show that kind of courage.

She refused to give up her seat on a segregated bus. On December 1, 1955 in Montgomery, Alabama a bus driver ordered Rosa to give up her seat in the colored section to a white passenger, after the white section was filled. She refused to give up her seat.

Her determination and fierce fire was to stand tall within her rights as a human being. She showed courage that day. The United States called her "The First Lady of Civil Rights"

She changed the way the world looked at American Civil Rights. What if she was not brave that day? It only takes one time to stand up for your rights and the rights of others.

Strength and courage is a soldier leaving his family to serve his or her country. They show courage when they are overseas walking the front lines to defend our country. The real strength comes when they return home and they need to carry on in such a different environment. Strength comes when they are up against evil and must stop it.

Courage is a police officer, like my brother Mark, who puts his life on the line every day. Thank you, Mark, for your service. It could be a fireman or woman putting on their uniform and protecting their city and their community from harm's way.

Strength and courage can be getting up in front of a room full of people and giving a speech for the first time.

Courage could be choosing to do what is right when everyone is doing wrong. For some, courage could be just getting out of bed.

Your courage can change people's hearts. The influence you have on people can change their thought process and decide to follow Christ.

There are benefits to having courage. Having courage and strength can change a nation. It can change how our population looks at life.

You can be that change.

There are risks that come with having strength and courage. Sometimes it means loss of one's life or a sacrifice you were not ready for. Maybe it will be a change that happens to you that you did not even see coming. But God is with you and he will never leave your side.

Have you had to do something in your life that would change the way you live your life? What was it?

Risks can make us stronger human beings. Don't be paralyzed by fear. It will only hold you back from what you are meant to be.

Live a life with courage; live a life with strength. Live a life with love and wisdom. To live a **crazy courageous** life every day may seem crazy but it is worth it.

Peter from the Bible is a man who took risks. The story of Peter is a true story of personal growth and strength. Peter was a fisherman who was called by Jesus to follow him. Jesus was looking for real people who could be changed by his love. So, Peter follows Jesus and became one of his disciples. After Jesus was crucified and died on the cross, it was up to Peter and the remaining disciples to be Jesus's witnesses and to spread God's message of love and forgiveness. Peter went to Jerusalem and Rome and talked to men, women and children about Jesus and his love for the people. He took risks by speaking in the courtyard to the common people. He was put in jail for his faith. Every day Peter put his life on the line to be a witness and tell of God's love. Peter spoke freely and bravely about Jesus Christ and that Jesus was the Messiah. Peter showed great courage and obedience to Jesus and in doing so Peter changed the hearts and minds of people. What a crazy courageous stand he made.

Another brave and courageous man from the Bible was Daniel. He was taken captive and deported to Babylon by King Nebuchadnezzar. Daniel had great wisdom and was obedient to God even though he was sent to serve in a foreign land where his faith would be tested. Daniel would serve for seventy years for four different kings. The first king was King Nebuchadnezzar. He was the king of Babylon. Along with Daniel, were his friends Hananiah, Mishael and Azariah. These four men were sent to serve under the king.

Daniel 1:3-7

Then the king ordered Ashpenaz, Chief of his court officials, to bring in some of the Israelites from the royal family and the nobility-- young men without any physical defect, handsome, showing aptitude for every kind of learning, well informed, quick to understand, and qualified to serve in the king's palace. He was to teach them the language and literature of the Babylonians. The king assigned them a daily amount of food and wine from the king's table. They were to be trained for three years; and, after that, they were to enter the king's service. Among these were people from Judah: Daniel, Hananiah, Mishael and Azariah. The chief official gave Daniel's three friends new names: to Hananiah, he renamed Shadrach; to Mishael, he renamed Meshach; and to Azariah, he renamed Abednego.

King Nebuchadnezzar wanted to change everything about these men. The king wanted men he could easily govern. King Nebuchadnezzar changed their names and took away their clothes so they would look like Babylonians. Have you ever felt like you had to change who you were to fit in a group or to be accepted? Daniel and his friends did not want to serve under the king and his rules, but knew it was God's will.

If you stay strong in your faith and obedient to God what you wear or become on the outside will not matter. Your faith and your commitment to God from within will keep you strong.

The first challenge these men faced was the eating and drinking of the king's food and wine. Daniel, Shadrach, Meshach and Abednego did not want to eat the king's food because it was unclean and anything that was sacrificed by other gods was not to be eaten. Daniel and his friends forbid to eat it.

They stayed faithful to God and came out stronger then the men who did eat the food and drank the wine. Showing strength in what you believe in will carry you through the hard times.

During the time that Daniel and his friends served King Nebuchadnezzar, they stayed faithful to their God. The king had a dream that puzzled him so much that he wanted it interpreted. He threatened his wise men and advisors with death if they could not interpret the dream. In staying faithful, Daniel and his friends would pray to their God that the mystery of the king's dreams would be revealed. Daniel revealed it perfectly.

Daniel 2:27- 28

    Daniel replied, "No wise men, enchanter, magician or diviner can explain to the king the mystery he has asked about; but there is a God in heaven who reveals mysteries. He has shown King Nebuchadnezzar what will happen in days to come.

Daniel 2:47-49

    The king said to Daniel, "Surely your God is the God of Gods and the Lord of kings and a revealer of mysteries, for you were able to reveal this mystery. Then the king placed Daniel in a high position and lavished many gifts on him. He made him ruler over the entire province of Babylon and placed him in charge of all its wise men. Moreover, at Daniel's request the king appointed Shadrach, Meshach and Abednego administrators over the province of Babylon, while Daniel himself remained at the royal court.

    People will doubt you and your faith. Situations will challenge you, and your faith will be tested. After Daniel and his three friends became highly regarded administrators under King Nebuchadnezzar, their faith was tested once again. The king had a ninety-foot tall statue built of himself and placed in the center of the city and demanded that all the people worship and bow down to the statue.

Shadrach, Meshach and Abednego were found guilty of not worshiping the King's ninety- foot high statue and they were ordered to be put into a fiery furnace.

Daniel 3:17-18

If we are thrown into the blazing furnace, the God we serve is able to save us from it; and he will rescue us from your hand, O King. But even if he does not, we want you to know, king, that we will not serve your gods or worship the image of gold you have set up.

Can you imagine the courage these men had to have, and the faith in God to stand before the king and go against the king's command?

Have you ever had to confront someone in a time where you were being asked to do something you knew was wrong? Were you afraid of the outcome or the retaliation? Did you stand strong through it or give in?

In this situation, the three men were asked to do something that was against their beliefs. The God they served sent an angel to rescue them; and, in this act, it showed the king that Shadrach, Meshach and Abednego's God was worthy of praise. They were not burned at all in the fiery furnace. Again and again in the book of Daniel, are stories of faith and obedience to God and the downfall of when you don't obey God.

Eventually Nebuchadnezzar humbled himself and acknowledged the God of Daniel as the ruler over all.

The second king was King Belshazzar, the son of King Nebuchadnezzar. He was an arrogant ruler who did as he pleased. One night he gave a banquet to a thousand of his nobles. The king ordered them to drink from the gold and silver goblets and while drinking, King Belshazzar praised the gods of gold, silver, bronze, iron, wood and stone. It was then that writing on the wall appeared before King Belshazzar and his nobles. The writing was unable to be interpreted. The king was perplexed and summoned Daniel to interpret the writing.

Daniel told the king that because he did not humble himself under God and worshipped other gods that his life will end and his kingdom will be divided. It was that very night that King Belshazzar was killed by a new king named King Darius.

King Darius began the rule over Babylon and employed Daniel who was now over 80 years old as an administrator of the kingdom.

Daniel 6: 3-9

Now Daniel so distinguished himself among the administrators and the satraps (governors) by his exceptional qualities that the king planned to set him over the whole kingdom.

At this, the administrators and the satraps tried to find grounds for charges against Daniel in his conduct of government affairs; but they were unable to do so. They could find no corruption in him because he was trustworthy and neither corrupt nor negligent. Finally these men said, "We will never find any basis for charges against this man Daniel unless it has something to do with the law of his God."

So the administrators and the satraps went as a group to the king and said "O King Darius, live forever! The royal administrators, prefects, satraps, advisers and governors have all agreed that the king should issue an edict and enforce the decree that anyone who prays to any god or man during the next thirty days, except to you, O King, shall be thrown into the lion's den. Now, O King, issue the decree and put it in writing so that it cannot be altered-- in accordance with the laws of Medes and Persians, which cannot be repealed." So, King Darius put the decree in writing.

Being a man of faith and obedience to God, Daniel did not follow this rule. He continued to pray to his God.

Daniel 6: 11

Then these men went as a group and found Daniel praying and asking God for help.

Now King Darius has to follow the law he put in place and put Daniel, his best advisor, into the Lion's Den. This upset King Darius very much, because he did not want to enforce this law when he realized Daniel would be put to death.

Daniel 6: 16

So the king gave the order, and they brought Daniel and threw him in the lion's den. The king said to Daniel, "May your God, whom you serve continually rescue you!"

Daniel 6:18-19

Then the King Darius returned to his palace and spent the night without eating and without any entertainment being brought to him. And he could not sleep. At the first sight of dawn, the king got up and hurried to the lion's den.

When he came near the den, he called to Daniel in an anguished voice. "Daniel, servant of the living God, has your God, whom you serve continually, been able to rescue you from the lion? "Oh King, live forever! My God sent his angles and he shut the mouths of the lions. They have not hurt me, because I was found innocent in his sight. Nor have I ever done any wrong before you, O King."

The best way to influence non- Christians is to work diligently and responsibly. How well do you represent God in your life or in your job? In making good decisions in your life, you will find enemies and people that want to be better than you and will stop at nothing to get there. People will always try to find fault in you and use it against you. It is your faith and obedience to God and reading his Word that will get you through it.

Daniel risked it all in this moment to stand by God in the truth. What Daniel showed was not only from within himself but that kind of courage comes from God and your faith in him. Daniel made it out alive and his faith was even stronger. He also showed King Darius and the people of Babylon that his God is the only God to serve. So Daniel helped to rule, Babylon the country he entered as a captive and he boldly stood for God and God rewarded him.

In your life, where have you seen your faith be tested like Daniels? We serve an amazing God, but not everyone agrees or likes the idea of God being in control.

What risks are we willing to take in the world today? How do you compare yourself to Daniel or any other person I have mentioned? What risks have you been through or have taken?

What risks do you take in your marriage to keep it strong? What risks do you take in your life to stand up for what is right? What risks are you willing to take for the truth?

Will you call on God and ask for help or will you hide behind the world?

Daniel showed no anger or revenge. He just believed in God and never gave up. Imagine your faith and the things you are up against. What if you could change someone's life by showing commitment to God, by being that example of what it means to live by faith?

When you live your life with strength and live a **CRAZY COURAGOUS** life, you show others there is something different about you. I promise you, you will come out a stronger person.

What is your trial right now in your life?

Is it your marriage? Do you talk things out with your spouse? Are you honest with each other?

Is it your job? No job can make you happy; you have to choose to be happy.

Maybe it is your children or a family member that is your challenge in life? Children are a blessing but they can drain us and push us to our limits. Write out what struggles you are going through. Remember love your family and your friends through the hard times. They are learning from you.

Are you going through a physical or mental challenge? I know pain can be depressing and exhausting. You want the pain to end and you wonder how or will I get through this. I know prayer works and you are not alone. Your pain is real and I know that. God has a plan and a reason for your life. Hold onto your faith and don't give up. Take it one minute at a time.

Whatever it is you are going through, ask yourself; "am I being honest with myself? Am I praying to God? Am I trying to understand the truth and obey God?" Imagine your life and the changes that could be made if you lived by truth.

Consider Daniel if he did not stand for his beliefs and truth, then would he have really made an impact on the kings and the country they ruled?

First believe in yourself, and believe **anything is possible.**

Philippians 4:13

I can do all things through Christ which strengthened me.

There is no perfect spouse, children or family member. The world tries to convince us that there is perfect out there, if we could just get there. But if we are always trying to be something we are not, then you will miss what is right in front of you.

Things can be good for someone in the moment but that does not mean they don't have struggles. Everyone handles life and struggles differently. We are all unique people and God made us that way. It is about living a life with courage and not being afraid to be strong. In life, we all go through ups and downs. Sometimes we are prepared for the challenges that lay ahead.

Sometimes we are not prepared and we have to be strong and courageous through it. I know for me, growing up with a sister with mental and physical disabilities helped me see life in a different way. As I said earlier, she made me stronger and more sensitive to how I wanted to live my life.

After my parents' divorce was over and finalized I started to move on in life. I was still dating Chris.

Chris went to college and he was making a way for his future. He went to school full time and studied for many hours. Any spare time he had (which wasn't much), he worked in a warehouse to earn money to pay for tuition and for gas to drive to school. He sometimes had to sell his favorite music CD's and jeans for the next semester's tuition. He also gave plasma several times per week for cash just so he could get lunch or get gas to get back home from school. He also drove an old car without air conditioning (in Phoenix!). The sacrifices he made to go to college were crazy.

He went through some hard times but he never complained. He knew there would be a better end to this. He knew what he had to do to get through these times. I really admire him for that. In 1999, he graduated from college and that same year Chris asked me to marry him. The following year, we were married. I met him on a roller coaster ride when I was fifteen. I knew from the moment I met him that he was my soulmate.

It is hard to put into words. I just felt peace and a sense of he would understand me for the rest of my life. But little did I know what it took to be married and how to be a wife? We had the normal struggles that all married people go through.

Shortly after we got married, Chris's parents separated after 33 years of marriage. Here we go again with more confusion and separation of our family. This is not a book about divorce by any means, but it is important for you to understand how decisions and choices can affect your life and other people's lives too. Chris's parents divorced in 2001. Now we both understood each other's feeling of the loss of that family connection. We were building a life together and all the exciting things that come in a new marriage, but we felt this disconnection between our families.

It was a hard time for us. But there was nothing we could do except stay strong in our marriage and stay close to each other. Not every day was easy.

During the summer of 2001, we got a puppy, a Labrador retriever. We named him Job. He was so cute and really made us happy with the unconditional love he gave us. It was fun having a dog. Good parent training. (LOL)

Life seemed okay working and living life until on that tragic day of September 11, 2001 when our nation was attacked. I was at work when I saw it on the news.

I could not even begin to understand why this had happened. I know there have been other attacks on our nation and plenty of wars, but this one hit home.

It was one of the most evil things I had ever seen. I wrote a poem about that day and it goes like this;

What would make a person do such a thing? Terror and Destruction, what to prove you are king? Life will never be the same. The secret hands behind it all, they will not break us down or break anymore walls. Playing with fire, playing with guns, all it does is gets the job done of ending innocent lives. A coward behind the mass destruction, there was no time to say goodbye, a little girl wondering why? As the people of New York City sit at their desks, next thing they know, there is an explosion in their chest. So many lives vanished away. So help them God, it's time to pray.

It changed our nation and the people in it. People's lives were never the same.

That day courage was found and strength was ignited.

In 2003, Chris decided to go back to school. He was accepted into PA.school. He was so excited, but knew the next two years would be very crazy and he would endure a lot.

So the journey began for us. I worked a full time job at a newspaper selling advertising and he started school. It was a two year program and we were ready. I supported the family and worked so he did not have to; and, besides that, he could not work a fulltime job as school was full time.

In 2004, I ran my first half-marathon and I never felt better crossing the finish line. I did something all by myself. I trained very hard for that run and felt proud of myself. During the race I had not felt the best. I was sick and just wanted to eat. Little did I know I was pregnant with our first child?

Changes were coming our way. I worked and Chris was in school. We were busy. When I was about five months pregnant, I was let go from my job. I was given no notice. I went into work and was told they were restructuring. I was devastated. It changed things for us. There was no warning.

This was a challenging time for us. Chris was working so hard with school and I was at home trying to look for work. I was going to have a baby in a few months. No one would hire me, knowing I was about to have a baby. We had no income to survive off of.

Late in the summer of 2004, our little Liam was born. He was so cute and precious. I was a mother now. Nothing meant more to me than Chris and Liam. We knew we had struggles, but we kept the faith and knew we would be okay. We had some family support, but it was a hard time for us. Chris worked night and day at school for two years with no break at all. He had to put a lot aside personally to get through this program. He was doing it for us so we could have a better life and I could take care of Liam. I finally got a job after Liam was about 2 months old and worked to support the family while Chris finished school. He graduated in June 2005. Liam was almost one year old.

When Chris found a good job I was able to stay home with Liam. About a year later, I was pregnant with our second child. Life was good and things seemed to calm down a little.

In 2007, Luke was born. He was the funniest little kid. He made us all laugh daily. That first year with two boys was a lot of fun. Watching Liam grow up and be the little man of the house while Luke was my baby. In the summer of 2008, we decided to put our house up for sale and buy a new home.

Well, we sold our home within seven days, bought a new home and found out I was pregnant all within the same week. Talk about crazy timing.

Crazy times can make you be stronger and have courage. We were having our home built and I was raising two boys and pregnant with our third.

In November 2008, my husband and I were shopping at the store with our children when I got a call from my mother. The reason for her calling me was to tell me that my grandmother died suddenly. I was devastated. Her name was Marilyn Rae Kell. She was an amazing woman with a strong personality. Out of everyone I have ever hugged in my entire life, by far, she was the best hugger ever. When we would hug, we just fit perfectly around each other. I was so sad about her sudden death because I did not know, with this third pregnancy, if I was having a boy or a girl. I was not able to tell her before she died that I was having a girl. I named her Madeline Rae after my grandmother and just felt like my daughter would be strong like her great-grandmother. My daughter is one strong little girl for sure.

I was so sad she did not get to meet her great-grandmother. We just never know when our time is up and so that is why it is so important to tell people how you feel and tell them you love them.

Life went on, and in 2009, I had my daughter. Life was good. The first year of Madeline's life was filled with sleepless nights and the joys of raising three wonderful children. But, in 2010, just when you think all is good with your children something crazy happens. Madeline and I were going, out one summer night in June off to the store for some shopping. I needed a few things and loved having her with me. I got in the car and headed out the driveway and, as I turned my head, I saw Madeline's face. I knew what was happening to Madeline because I often saw the same look on my twin sister's face. Madeline was having a seizure. I have never been so scared in my life. Chris was home and heard my screams and helped me bring Madeline into the house. Chris immediately called 911. Chris was amazing--I, on the other hand, was a mess. Madeline was my precious little girl and I feared I was going to lose her. I began to pray, "Dear God, please don't take my baby." The ambulance rushed us to the hospital where the doctors ran many tests on Madeline. After the tests were done, the Doctors determined that Madeline had a febrile seizure which was brought on by a high fever.

It was rather strange because, before I headed off to the store, I informed Chris that Madeline felt hot. We had been outside playing in the sun. When we came inside, Madeline felt warm. I thought to myself, "Maybe she is teething." So I gave her some children's Motrin.

That was a very scary time, and, you would think because I saw my sister have seizures, I would be stronger and calm. But I was not. I had a fear that my daughter would have continuous seizures and resulting in brain damage. I was very protective of Madeline and grew even closer to her after that day.

In 2011, I was ready to train for another half-marathon. I wanted to beat my time from the first half-marathon I ran. I knew that after having three children, I needed to find "me" again, and that is when a whole new journey began for me. I did beat my time and it felt AWESOME!

Then, between 2012 and 2013, my life changed again. There were a great deal of changes and challenges for me and my family. I was raising my three children while working a part- time job at a gym. I worked in the childcare department and was able to take my children with me to work. I also worked for a jewelry company selling jewelry and having jewelry parties. It was a fun time and I learned a great deal from both jobs.

It was in March of 2012 when I decided, after five years of working at the gym, to quit and focus more on working for the jewelry company and raise my children. Also, I have been writing for over 23 years and have written many songs, poems and many children's books. It is a huge passion of mine. I knew I wanted to take my writing further.

In May 2012, my mother went into the hospital for some leg pain. The doctors discovered that she had blood clots on both her lungs. It was a very scary time for both of us. My mother is my very best friend and I could not imagine life without her.

My children and I visited my mother while she was in the hospital. One day when I went I went to see my mother; I stopped at the gift shop to get my children a snack. I saw the cutest purse I have ever seen there in the gift shop. I have always had a passion-or maybe an addiction- to purses. Just like my Grandma Kell.

I just knew I needed that purse so I purchased it. I took it up with me to my mom's room. When she saw the bag that the purse was in, "What did you buy?" I said, "A beautiful purse." My mom knew me really well and just made a face until she saw the purse. She said "That is really cute." Buying that purse really changed my life.

It seemed like I was having one challenge after another. June of 2012, our dog, Job, passed away. We were all so very sad. Job was an amazing dog who showed nothing but love and loyalty. Shortly after that happened, in August, I had to go to the dentist to get all four wisdom teeth pulled out. I thought it would be no big deal. I have never had any major surgery on my mouth before, but I figured I would be fine. This kind of procedure goes on every day. I was a little nervous but thought nothing bad could happen. I had all four wisdom teeth taken out and the dentist said the bottom left side was very deep. The dentist had a hard time getting that tooth out. He thought that he might have hit a nerve while taking out that tooth. I was in so much pain.

I couldn't eat for two weeks because of the pain in my jaw and I could hardly open my mouth. I could only open my mouth enough for soft foods and soups. To make things worse, Luke was starting kindergarten the following Monday after my surgery. I was not able to even talk to him to wish him a great first day.

After weeks of follow -up visits to the dentist, he confirmed that he had hit a nerve and that it might take months, or maybe up to a year, for the numbness to go away.

Well, it's now 2016 as I am writing this and I still have a numb chin and mouth. I had to learn to eat, to talk, to kiss and smile all over again. I didn't understand that it took so many muscles to do these simple things. I felt deeply about what had happened to me. I wanted my mouth to feel normal. I wanted to smile and talk normal. I was angry! I also wanted to be able to kiss my kids and my husband and actually feel the kiss. My mouth was so numb that I could not feel very much. But, for some reason, my heart started to change when I began to realize that maybe this ordeal was going to turn out to be a beautiful blessing. Life isn't perfect and things that happened to you in your life can be a growing and positive experience.

It's how you grow from the experience. I went from a deep depression thinking I will never be able to talk the same. I will never want to talk in front of people because I always thought I spoke funny with half my mouth feeling numb all the time. But something inside me changed. I knew I could get out of my depression and rise above it. I had to, to keep living.

I told myself I could let this beat me or I would beat it. So I overcame my fear and knew that I would be okay. Remember when I told you in the summer of 2012 I bought a purse, that purchase changed my life and inspired me to start my own purse company. The purse I bought in the gift shop was very unique and cute.

Where ever I went people would ask, "Where did you get that adorable purse?" I would go to the store or my children's sport events and I would get stopped all the time. I would tell my mother about all the excitement my purse generated she said , "Well, why don't you sell purses?" I thought that sounded like so much fun. So the more I contemplated the idea, the faster the dream came to life. My mother helped me with the name of my business. I wanted to have the word" Pinky "in the name. My Grandma Kell, loved purses; and, when I was little, I would play in her closet all the time and try out each of her purses. You could say she loved purses as much as, or even more than me. This is where my passion for purses came to life.

My Grandma Kell was born with a pink pigment on her skin. So her mother nicknamed her "Pinky." When I was thinking of names for my business, I wanted to honor my grandmother because she was such a strong woman and she would have been so proud of me for doing something like this. I also wanted to show my children that you can do anything if you put your heart into it. So I came up with "Pinkys Got Purses." I had started my own company.

I was getting started. I build my website and registered my company with the state. In November of 2012, my mother and I got in her car and drove to California to purchase inventory. I was so excited for the shopping. I was like a kid in a candy store.

Driving with my mother and learning how to run a business was amazing. I could not thank her enough for all her help and advice in this new adventure I was on. I stopped working for the jewelry company because I wanted to concentrate on my passion for purses. As I was building my business and raising three children, I was reminded that life still carries on.

As I was building my business and raising children, life still happened, right? In December, my grandpa Lindsey passed away. It is always hard losing someone in your family. My Grandma Lindsey had a hard time with this of course. They had been together for so long. He was such a great man. My grandparents met in Australia during World War II. It was a love story that would take them through life raising seven boys and living a great life. Later that same year my husband's grandpa passed away.

The stories they told us, we will always remember and the legacy that we hold dear to our hearts is something we want to pass down to our children.

Now it was a new year, in 2013 my husband and I joined a soccer league to get healthy and have some fun doing something together. That experience lasted five minutes for me. Five minutes into the game I was trying to stop somebody from scoring a goal and I broke my foot.

I guess I was not supposed to play soccer. When I went to the first doctor, he did not diagnose the problem with my foot right. I was walking on my foot and it was not healing. The second doctor I went to discovered it was broken. I was in a walking boot for eight months.

It was quite an experience. Driving was fun with my left foot. That experience taught me patience. I'm a busybody and I don't sit still very well and let me tell you how much that boot made me sit still and I did not like it.

Things that seem so big to you at the time are really just ways to make you stronger. I know that my mouth and the experience of it going numb have not been easy and I had to figure out how to grow from that experience. Also the breaking of my foot slowing me down is nothing compared to what others have gone through. Maybe these experiences are making me stronger for the future. I know that my sad days are nothing compared to what some people have seen or gone through.

The war in some people's minds can be tormenting. The pain of cancer or abuse is not something you wake up one morning and feel normal or at peace with. There is real pain in the world. Some people struggle with addiction and cannot break free from it.

The old saying what does not kill us makes us stronger is a great metaphor and can be true in some situations, but real life happens to real people and the more we are aware of the struggles and the real issues, the more we can help and be there for each other.

I know where I am today with all I have been through has made me who I am. The struggle of having a sister with mental and physical disabilities is huge for me. It changed everything. Seeing and feeling the pain of what divorce does to a family was hard and the healing is an everyday process. Life is not easy but being a Christian, wife, mother, business owner and a writer has totally made me who I am today.

I would not trade any of the trials or situations because it is what brought me to where I am today. It is what shapes me to who God wants me to be.

In 2015, struggles came again to our family. Both my husband and I had lost family that was very close to us. It was a hard year. My husband and I both lost very special people in our lives. Erin, who is my husband's cousin passed way Easter weekend. She had been fighting cancer for three years. I first met Erin when she was a little girl. During my years of dating Chris, I got close to everyone in his family. Erin was quiet and much younger than me. Chris's aunt and uncle moved to Washington a few years after I met Chris so Erin was living in Washington.

It was later when she graduated from high school that she decided to move back to Arizona to go to college. This is when I got closer to Erin. When we had children, Erin was a great babysitter us. She loved our children so much. Erin was going to college to become a nurse. It was during her struggle with cancer, that I became even closer to her. I spent more time with her and we started having movie nights. We would hang out and watch some great movies.

Life was busy and she was getting weaker so our movie night did not happen very often. We were planning to watch a new movie that was coming out sometime in March but she was too weak by then. She passed away April 4, 2015. I wrote a poem for her and read it at her funeral. That was a very hard day. She will be missed and I know she is looking down on us from heaven.

Celebration of Life

There is a celebration of life today.
We had so much more we wanted to say.
Her life was filled with laughter and love
and we know she is smiling down on us from above.
Remember how important one's life purpose can
mean and what their smile can bring.
Erin left behind her courage, her strength.
Erin left behind a message we all must embrace.
She left it behind so we could carry it on.
We are all God's children, we must keep the bond.
She was so strong and so courageous and had a smile
so bright. Where she went, she did not need to have
courage or strength it was already within her sight.
She went to be with God who is strength who is
courageous and who is kindness and love. She left all
of that for us to carry-on so we may be kind so we may
be courageous so we may have strength and so we will
never feel she is gone. Erin left her footprints, her
mark in this life, may we lead by example
and never give up the fight.
Keep living, keep loving, keep smiling.
We love you Erin and we miss you.

I miss her so much and if I could just hug her one more time or say I love you one more time. She is in peace and has no pain.

My uncle also passed away the same year. He suffered from cancer as well. Cancer takes your life away. I don't understand this disease. It has taken so many people. For three years, he struggled and went through so much pain. The last three years of my uncle's life, I made sure I constantly told him that I loved him. I was so glad that he knew it too. I always told him he was in my prayers. Chris and I took our children to visit him in August. He knew he did not have much time and he wanted us to visit him before he got weaker. He was a very adventurous man and full of life. I know my aunt is still hurting and has to find the will and the way to move on. It is really hard for her. She lost her best friend and partner for life. The one person she wanted to grow old with is gone. I wrote the following poem for him and I wish I could have read it to him before he passed away.

The Meaning of Life

The meaning of life cannot be measured by just the touch of your hand.

The meaning of life cannot be measured by just the presence of your smile.

The meaning of life and all its joy and with all its sorrow.

We must hold on today for we don't know if we have tomorrow.

Through the miracles of life and through the sadness of pain.

Knowing your life mattered and that we will never be the same.

Love shapes us.

Kindness grows us.

Faith heals us.

See- - sad things are going to happen in your life. There will be trials and tribulations. There will be people that disappoint you in your life.

There will be death or divorce and evil people, but those people and situations can only make us stronger and fight through it with strength and courage. Life will bring you to unexpected places and through difficult circumstances; but if you believe you are not alone and also believe you will get through it, then you will. Have faith in God. Let what you are going through change you and guide you. **Let it grow you**.

This chapter was very long and dedicated to my trials in life, my comebacks, the people that have gone before me, and to the future that lies ahead.

It's about living with **STRENGTH** and living **CRAZY COURAGEOUS!!!!**

Chapter Eight

I Vow To Let LOVE Lead Me and Leave the Hate Behind

What is love?

Love is a feeling of strong or constant affection for a person or something. Okay, so that is Webster's definition for love, but what is love really? Love is seeing beyond the hate. Love is selfless and giving. Love is never giving up. Love is in your smile. Love is seeing someone for who they really are. Love heals people. The love you give someone can shape them forever.

We all need and want love. No one wants to be unloved. It is an empty feeling.

Love cannot remain by itself-- it has no meaning. Love has to be put into action and that action is service.

Mother Teresa

John 13:34
I give you a new command:
Love each other, you must love each other as I have loved you.
All people will know that you are my followers if you love each other.

When we love one another we spread kindness like a wildfire. Let love grow inside you. Love makes you feel good. God is the essence of Love.

So why is there so much hate?

What is hate? Hate is a very strong feeling of dislike. Hate can also be intense hostility and aversion usually deriving from fear, anger, or sense of injury. Why do we have so much hate in our world?

Everyone wants to be right or be on top so to get there you have to pull people down. People are self-seekers and self-involved so much that they miss the importance of life and the meaning behind it. Maybe you are hurting from hate in your life? Has someone hurt you? Have you hurt someone? When we feel hate our walls are up. Hate is malicious.

Some people are filled with anger and hate so much that they become dangerous to our society. They become virulent which means full of hate and anger. You can list the reasons for hate but why, we know what they are. If we are for ourselves only then we are not for others. If we cannot see that everyone goes through different struggles and that everyone is the same on the inside then you will not get the kindness that is needed to win in the outside world.

You might have walls up because someone hurt you. You are defensive and standoffish so love comes harder. To show love it might be hard and difficult, but it is not impossible. If you let God's love grow in you and you let it lead you then you can show love. In doing this, it will not only fill up your emptiness but it will allow you to give love to others even if it is hard.

1John 4:16
God is love. Whoever lives in love lives in God, and God in him.

I do know hate exists. It is out there and we have to fight against it.

I believe that the core of your heart and the core of your soul is what you're supposed to resonate in this world.

How do you love above hate and evil? It is easy to judge somebody in this world. It's easy to target a person that might not look the right way or act the right way. Really what is the right way to look? What does it look like? That is what is so amazing about God, he made us all different. He made us all unique so we can all learn from each other and use each other's talents and thoughts and abilities.

Love and kindness does not judge based on rich or poor, black or white. Love and kindness does not judge on man or woman or young or old. Love and kindness has no judgment on you it just gives.

Don't you know you will be judged for your hate? Maybe you don't care. Hate is a huge problem in our world today. You see it in the news every day. Now, hate can be a matter of opinion. There are things we hate in this world. I hate black coffee but that will not change the world or affect anyone really. I hate violence, racism and terrorism. These acts of hate really change the way the world looks at life.

Life is not just simply life, it is living, breathing human beings that matter and who want to stand and live for something.

Those issues are real and affect people's lives. Hating someone for the clothes they wear or the person they love is not a reason to hate them. Our world is filled with so many different people but just because we are different does not give you the right to hate them.

We are all going to have different ideas of how we think the world should work but if your hate is destroying the common good for all mankind then that is the hate I am talking about.

Is there evil in your mind or in your heart?

God did not die on the cross for us so we could spread evil. He died to spread **LOVE.**
Whether it be gossip or talking bad about someone or judging them it is all the same evil.
You must love above evil and judgment.
There will be days that you feel that the world is on top of you and that the hate is just too much.
That's when you surrender your soul. You give up control and let the Holy Spirit guide you. That's when you release all fear of falling and failing and give it to God. You have to believe in yourself and that God lives in you.

There are times we try to take on the world as if we know what we're doing. The amazing thing is, even when you think you're in control, you're really not in control of anything.

God placed the moon and the stars where they belong and he put you where you belong it might not be where you thought you would be or where you would go but that's where he wants you and you can fight against it or embrace it.

Jesus showed us the perfect way to show kindness and to be kind to people. He let every person know that they were worth something. It did not matter who you were. He showed love and kindness to everyone.

In our world today of hate and fighting, kindness seems scarce and almost impossible to be shown. I have a hard time with that concept because we all go through life with different struggles and our own pain and if we were just a little more patient and showed kindness we might be a happier society.

Luke 6:31

"Do to others as you want them to do to you."

Learn to love more and leave the hate behind because hate is just a waste of time. It will eat you up and swallow you. The devil wants us to hate, he wants us to fall down. He can't wait for us to fall apart so he can defeat us. He wants this so he can show us that evil and hate are a better solution to life than love. Because when you love and give, sometimes there are sacrifices and challenges but the end result is amazing.

Kindness is not selective; people are selective on who they share their kindness with.

Let us spread kindness.

Chapter Nine

I Vow To LOVE

Above

Evil and Judgment

We wonder why there is so much hate in our world. We wonder why people are always fighting against each other instead of learning and growing with each other.

There is starvation everywhere you look and I don't just mean starving from food.

People are starving for love, starving for attention and starving just to belong. There are wars over so many different things in every country.

Children are seeing things at a younger age these days. This puts ideas in their minds and thoughts that they cannot handle yet. There is drug abuse and child abuse that seems to never go away.

Evil means morally wrong or causing harm to someone.

Today, our society seems to think that morals don't stand for much anymore. It's not bad if you tell a couple of lies or don't follow all the rules. The things that we teach our children not to do, we do them anyway. We teach our children to be kind, we teach them not to judge, we teach our children to share, and we teach them not to hate. Yet, our words quickly disappear. There's no action behind our words. There's no proof by our actions to truly teach them how to love.

LOVE

1 John 4:8

    Whoever does not love does not know God, because God is love.

Paul talks about love in a way that can change you forever.

Corinthians 13: 1-13

    If I speak with human eloquence and angelic ecstasy but don't love, I'm nothing but a creaking of a rusty gate. If I speak God's word with power, revealing all his mysteries and making everything plain as day, and if I have faith that's says to a mountain "jump" and it jumps, but I don't have love, I'm nothing. If I give everything I own to the poor and even go to the stake to be burned as a martyr, but I don't love, I've gotten nowhere. So no matter what I say, what I believe, and what I do, I'm bankrupt without love.

You can speak kindly but if you don't love, then what are you really doing. If you say, "Well, I give to the poor." That is good, but if you don't demonstrate love, then what are you really showing others and saying about yourself? This scripture is so important. You can say I will die for my family or for my faith, but if you don't show love through it all, then what are you showing people, what did you give?

What does judgment mean?

Luke 6:41

Why do you notice the little piece of dust in your friend's eye but don't notice the big piece of wood in your own eye.

Judgment is the ability to come to an opinion about things.

So, let's start with the first part of this definition. Judgment is an opinion. Your opinion on people or things is your opinion and no one else's. When you judge someone based on your feeling and not facts, sometimes you might be wrong. If you think about your decision and give yourself time and think things through, then you might make a good decision.

The truth about judgment is that whatever you are judging if you don't put much thought into it then you could be wrong. We all know when we judge someone by the way they act, look or the way they dress without even knowing the person, then your judgment is your opinion.

Unfortunately, people still judge people for the most, minute things. We judge for looks, how much money we have, where we are in our jobs, how we raise our kids or what car we drive.

Maybe you're judged for the way you look because it does not fit with society. We are judged for our faith; we are judged for who we love; or who we don't love.

We are all in a hurry these days and don't have time to think about why others do or say what they say. We just judge.

While Jesus walked the earth, he was judged for his works on this earth. He spoke to the lame and the blind. He gave to the weak; he gave to the poor; he did not judge them.

You can be humble within yourself and know that life is hard enough and that there's no room for evil and there's no room for judgment. We are all living, breathing human being just trying to make it in this world. If we can do it with kindness and love, then that is saying a lot about who we are.

Here is a story of how Jesus heals a blind man with no hesitation and no questions asked.

John 9:1-12

Jesus Heals the Man Who Was Born Blind

As he (Jesus) went along, he saw a man blind from birth.
His disciples asked him, "Rabbi, who sinned, this man or his parents, that he was born blind?"
"Neither this man nor his parents sinned," said Jesus, "but this happened so that the works of God might be displayed in him.
As long as it is day, we must do the works of him who sent me. Night is coming, when no one can work.
While I am in the world, I am the light of the world."
After saying this, he spit on the ground, made some mud with the saliva, and put it on the man's eyes.
"Go," he told him, "wash in the Pool of Siloam" (this word means "Sent"). So the man went and washed, and came home seeing. His neighbors and those who had

formerly seen him begging asked, "Isn't this the same man who used to sit and beg?"
Some claimed that he was. Others said, "No, he only looks like him." But he himself insisted, "I am the man."
"How then were your eyes opened?" they asked.
He replied, "The man they call Jesus made some mud and put it on my eyes. He told me to go to Siloam and wash. So I went and washed, and then I could see."
"Where is this man?" they asked him. "I don't know," he said.

John 9:13-16
     They brought to the Pharisees the man who had been blind. Now the day on which Jesus had made the mud and opened the man's eyes was a Sabbath. Therefore the Pharisees also asked him how he received his sight. "He put mud on my eyes," the man replied, "and I washed, and now I see." Some of the Pharisees said. "This man is not from God, for he does not keep the Sabbath."
But others asked, "How can a sinner do such miraculous signs?" So they were divided.

John 9: 18-25
     The Jews still did not believe that he had been blind and received his sight until they sent for the man's parents. "Is this your son?" They asked. "Is this the one you say was born blind? How it is that now he can see?"
"We know he is our son," the parents answered, "and we know he was born blind. But how he can see now, or who opened his eyes, we don't know. Ask him. He is of age; he will speak for himself." His parents said this because they were afraid of the Jews, for already the

Jews had decided that anyone who acknowledged that Jesus was the Christ would be put out of the synagogue. That was why his parents said, "He is of age; ask him." A second time they summoned the man who had been blind. "Give glory to God, they said. "We know this man is a sinner." He replied, "Whether he is a sinner or nor, I don't know. One thing I do know. I was blind and now I see!"

John 9:35-39

Jesus Teaches about Spiritual Blindness

Jesus heard that they had thrown him out, and when he found him, he said, "Do you believe in the Son of Man?" "Who is he, sir?" the man asked. "Tell me so that I may believe in him."
Jesus said, "You have now seen him; in fact, he is the one speaking with you."

Then the man said, "Lord, I believe," and he worshiped him.

Jesus said, "For judgment, I have come into this world so that the blind will see and those who see will become blind"

Jesus did not come to judge, but to heal and to show what true love is. Today, with all the social media, internet and TV, There is many avenues for evil and judgment to seep through to our hearts. It can manipulate your brain and make you see things in a critical, judgmental way. It is so huge that it's almost uncontrollable. We need to fill our hearts and minds with things that give us a more positive perspective of life and people. We can rise above what is put in front of us and choose to love people and choose not to judge. Take a moment and look at what or who you are judging. Look at what you are criticizing and look at what you're saying. If you would want that to be said about you then what does your character show?

What does your character stand for?

How can you change your environment to become less judgmental and have a more positive impact on your life and on those around you?

Don't let evil and judgment rule over your soul and take it over. It can be a very powerful dangerous thing.

Loving someone does not mean it's going to be easy. Loving and caring for people takes work and patience. Love can come in different stages and in different ways. We all go through our own seasons in our souls and we can all grow to be people of great character.

Kill them with kindness.

Romans 12: 9-20

    Love must be sincere. Hate what is evil; cling to what is good. Be devoted to one another in brotherly love. Honor yourself. Never be lacking in zeal; but keep your spiritual fervor, serving the Lord.

    Be joyful in hope, patient in affliction and faithful in prayer. Share with God's people who are in need. Practice hospitality.

    Bless those who persecute you; bless and do not curse. Rejoice with those who rejoice; mourn with those who mourn. Live in harmony with one another. Do not be proud, but be willing to associate with people of low position. Do not be conceited.

    Do not repay anyone evil for evil. Be careful to do what is right in the eyes of everyone. If it is possible, as far as it depends on you, live in peace with everyone. Do not take revenge, my friends, but leave room for God's wrath, for it is written: "It is mine to avenge; I will repay," says the Lord. On the contrary:

    "If your enemy is hungry, feed him; if he is thirsty, give him something to drink.

    I know this is a long verse but did you really read it. What was Paul trying to say? He was saying love above all; nothing else matters unless you love. Judgment will only keep you bitter and then no one wins.

Once, I was waiting in line at a coffee shop when a woman in front of me paid for her drink and walked away. As she did, her cane fell to the ground. I walked over to her to help her pick it up and said, "Can I help you?"

I picked it up and smiled. The lady looked at me with a sour look as if I had done something wrong to her. I thought to myself for a moment on what had happened and said well that was not very nice of her to look at me like that. Here I was trying to help her and she is mad at me for it. Maybe she was embarrassed and did not want anyone's help. While I was getting my drink, I thought, "Kill them with Kindness." Some people in this world will not accept kindness or caring people but that does not mean we give in or give up. We keep trying. It does not matter what others say or do; we should be kind no matter what.

That is not always easy to do. Sometimes we don't care to be nice. Just keep it to yourself then if you are having a bad day no sense making someone else have a bad day.

Luke 6: 27-28

"But I say to you who are listening, love your enemies. Do good to those who hate you, bless those who curse you, pray for those who are cruel to you."

I will show love even if it is hard and even if it seems like I get nothing back.

Chapter Ten

I Vow to LOVE when it just does not seem possible to Love

We have all been there, where we have had people in our life that have hurt us or that have been mean to us. Perhaps you were hurt as a child. Was it your parents that hurt you? Did you get hurt by a sibling or another family member?

Was it that somebody said something that left a mark on your soul? Could it be your situation runs deep and that it is hard to love? Do your circumstances make it hard to show love to others?

Maybe you have a spouse that cheated on you or has left you and you feel all alone. If you grew up in a home where love was not shown, you might have to learn how to express it to others. You might have walls up and it is hard for those walls to come down. I know for me, when my parents divorced it was really hard for me to show love because I was so confused on why they got divorced. To find out that their marriage did not work out made my heart very hard and cold. It was hard for me to show love, but I realized by not forgiving them cause me more pain. If you forgive people and learn how to love them, then the anger and the pain will not control you anymore. As I mentioned in chapter nine, which is well worth repeating, we teach our children not judge. We teach our children to share and not to hate. Yet, sometimes our words disappear. Many times there is no action behind our words.

Look at each one of these descriptions of what love is and spend a few moments thinking about them. Love is patient, love is kind. Why is love patient or kind? Love does not envy or boast and is not proud. What if our thoughts and actions were like this every day?

1 Corinthians 13:4-8

Love is patient, love is kind. It does not envy, it does not boast, it is not proud. It does not dishonor others, it is not self-seeking, it is not easily angered, it keeps no record of wrongs. Love does not delight in evil but rejoices with the truth. It always protects, always trusts, always hopes, and always perseveres. Love never fails.

What does it mean to love even if you think it is not possible?

One of the greatest love stories ever told and one of sacrifice is the crucifixion and death of Jesus Christ. He paid the ultimate price. He was beaten and mocked and put to death all because he loved us.

He knew he had done no wrong, but yet he went through the pain and suffering for us so we would be forgiven. He is our father. He showed the greatest gift of all. He gave us love. Unconditional love was freely given. To give that kind of love can be a risk. It is not always easy to give this kind of love to just anyone.

Sometimes it is even hard to give it to people we really love. Let me tell you though, putting it all out there can only make you stronger.

Loving someone even if it does not seem possible is a brave move. Sometimes we need to see what is behind that love. Maybe there is someone in your life who is so shut off from emotions that, when you try just a little, they look the other way.

I know for me there are people in my life who I love and I would love nothing more than that 100% love back. I know that to show love to someone could mean you don't always get it back or get it the way you wanted it, but then that is not true love for a person if you are doing something or giving of yourself to another person for something in return.

You need to know that you can love a person and want it back in return, but if you don't get it back, never give up on them or let go of your love for them. Maybe they need your love more than you need theirs.

I know this can be hard. Showing unconditional love can be a game changer for most people. Please don't misunderstand what I am saying here. You can show love and want it in return; but if you don't receive love back, don't hold a grudge. Give it to God and let him work on the relationship. Don't give up on those individuals but at the same time don't dwell on it either. There needs to be a balance with love and with your relationships. This is a lesson I am always wanting and trying to learn. In this day in age, things come very fast to us. Patience is not easy. If we slow down and take each day as it comes and each part of our journey on earth as it comes. We can grow in those moments. Slow down and see what is really in front of us.

It is very important to love yourself first and know that you have value. When we first know we love ourselves, then we can let go of the expectation of the impossible.

When you believe in yourself and know that you are not perfect but you are a gift from God and are full of value and that your life means something, then you know there is love out there to give and it is not impossible.

Loving when it does not seem possible means you love without judgment or condemning. It means you leave out the hate and the jealously. Love when it does not seem possible means you give without question and you love without compare. Love is possible by sharing your talents with people. Sharing with the poor and sharing your life and lending a hand not your wallet all the time. Love is smiling at your neighbors even if you don't agree with them or maybe you don't like them. It's okay. You don't have to like someone to show love. Love is giving your shirt off your back to a person in need. Love is a choice and when you love yourself then it seems easier to share it. Love is possible when we see strangers helping strangers. Love is possible when life's tragedies change your life or someone else's life. So, when you can step into someone's life and be that friend, for them you are showing and sharing your love.

Love is possible when you love someone for who they are not what they do. Love is possible when you accept reality and face what is before you. Love is putting other people first. Love is possible when we love ourselves for who we are and not what society wants us to be.

Love is possible if you believe that it is possible. There is meaning behind it. Love might be there for just a moment or for a lifetime. Either way, grab it, hold it, feel it and don't let go of it.

Love might be there for just a moment or a lifetime.

Chapter Eleven

I Vow To LOVE My Family, My Friends and My Enemies

You might think to love your family, your friends, and your enemies is easy. "Of course I love my family and friends." It can be hard to love your enemies for sure!!! But, in a lot of cases, loving family and friends can be just as hard, and sometimes even harder, then loving our enemies. Let me start first loving family.

Loving your family can have its ups and downs. I know that there are some of you, who are reading this, might be saying, "You don't know my family and what they have done to me?"

You are right. I don't know your story or maybe the hardship you have gone through. I know that there might be situations where you were really hurt or even to the point that maybe you don't talk to your family any more. I am sorry if that has happened to you. You might feel lost and confused because of that or you might feel relieved that the negative parts of your life are over. Whatever your situation is or was, you can always learn from it and grows.

I know for myself, family is very important to me because I know I have learned from them and I am still learning about them and myself every day. When my parents divorced, it broke my heart and my idea of what I thought family should be or look like. When I woke up and saw that my reality was different, I had to choose to forgive and love them no matter what.

If God loves me in spite of all my mistakes, then I should love my family in spite of all their mistakes. There will always be challenges with family but learning to LOVE through it will help you. Also giving it to God and let him carry your weight will allow you to not feel alone or feel the pain of it all.

Being honest with family is very important. When I look back on my childhood and see the way it was compared to the way I wanted it to be, I have no choice but to feel blessed for the way it was. I learned a lot and I am the woman I am today because of it.

Life shapes us and situations make us into the people we are. You can't look back and say if I would have only said this or done that then things would have been different, but you sometimes don't know until the situation is past.

If you compare where you are now in your life to where you wanted to be, you will go nowhere. I spent wasted hours thinking about what I wanted or where I wanted my life to go instead of really living my life. This hurt me because deep inside I know I can't go back to what I once wanted. I can't bring my parents back together. Things happen for a reason. So like I have said before you can let it break you or you can grow from the experience. I can only move forward and forgive and love. Friends are very important and they are sometimes our saving grace in life and your friends can be the true mirror of life. I have many friends that have come and gone in my life and they have all taught me something that I will carry along with me.

I wrote this following poem for all my friends.

The Meaning of Friendship

In life, we find friendships along the way.

Some are meant to go and some are meant to stay.

Friendship is the seed to a growing woman's heart.

We both feel it right from the start.

A friend is someone who does not care
what you look like, or

How crazy you might be; and we all know
I am a little crazy.

So, I am glad you are friends with me.

A friend is honest, loyal and strong;

And that is why we have been friends for so long.

Having a friend like you is a blessing beyond measure;

And it is a friendship I will always treasure.

Your friendship is rare and true and that is why

I LOVE YOU!

Thank you for the friendship, the laughter
and the love!!!

Friendships can teach us about ourselves. Friendships can fail us because we are real people and we are not all the same. We can think differently about things but one thing I have learned is if a friendship does not last, don't look at it as a bad thing. Maybe it was supposed to teach you something or show you where you need to go in life. Maybe it taught you about trust or letting go of something. The world is filled with so many people with so many different thoughts and ideas. It will be alright if some friendships come and go. Love the people in your life and love the friendships you have made. Learn to just love and leave the rest to GOD.

Don't be afraid to be open with people and be real. It is easier than trying to remember what you lied about or made up to look good. I like social media for the sharing and the fun videos and it has done some real good for people with bringing people closer. But it has also created hate, anger and jealousy. Don't make your life about what's on social media or in the public eye. It's what's inside your soul that is real. What is inside of your soul?

Let your soul burn bright, let your soul breath and know that while you are searching for LOVE it can be right in front of you in the real friendships you have in the real family you have. Open your arms to what might be scary but also be open to what is possible.

Proverbs 18:24

    Some friends may ruin you, but a real friend will be more loyal then a brother.

    Enemies-- we all have them. They are people that have maybe hurt us or hurt our family; and to you, they are enemies.

    Enemies want to destroy us and break us down. Some enemies can be changed by love and others are so far deep in evil that there is no coming back to reality. It might only be by the grace of God that our enemies can be saved. There are people in this world who don't care about anyone but themselves.

    These people show no remorse to any one's pain. These are people who have been hurt so bad that they are left numb to the real feeling of life or love. They are so blind to see what they have done or what they do to others. They may have been hurt as a child or as an adult; and they have that anger inside of them and the only way they feel better is to not let anyone in. They close off the true meaning to life and what it means to have love in their heart and forgiveness and truth.

You might feel alone because of the hurt that someone caused you and it weighs you down to where you don't want to love or be loved. People can be really mean sometimes and if you are holding all that inside your heart, then you can't fully grow as a person unless you forgive them and try to love again. We have all hurt someone and have been hurt by somebody. We have to break the cycle and love.

Allow me to assure you that suspicion and jealousy never helped any man in any situation.

— Abraham Lincoln

Abraham Lincoln was asked why he tried to make friends with his enemies, when he should be trying to destroy them. Lincoln replied "That he was destroying his enemies when he made them his friends. If you look for good in others you might find good in yourself. "

This is a great motto for life. Why let people get to you or get inside your soul when you can rise above it and show them kindness. If they don't respond to it then there was nothing lost in trying and hoping for an opportunity.

Courage is contagious. When a brave man takes a stand, the spines of others are stiffened.

–Billy Graham

Be courageous in love and forgive those who have hurt us. You will inspire others to love the unlovable.

CRAZY COURAGEOUS

Joshua 1:9

Be strong and courageous. Do not be terrified; do not be discouraged, for the Lord your God will be with you wherever you go.

We all have souls that are alive. Whether we use our souls to show and create love or hate is up to you. Our enemies get the best of us when we hate back. They win when we show hate back and then we are no different from them. If we fight back with justice and love then we have overcome the evil.

We all will die someday and the way we lived our lives will be remembered our actions will speak even if we can't. So leave your mark, leave your love, and leave your smile for someone else to carry on for you.

Vow to LOVE, love your family. Vow to LOVE, love your friends. Vow to LOVE, love your enemies.

Chapter Twelve

I Vow To LOVE Beyond Measure because Life is a Treasure

When a baby is born they are looked at like the most precious thing. Fragile and need 100% support. As that child grows they become more independent and no longer need that help. Somewhere along the way the treasure of life gets lost and how precious we really are is diminished. We as people lose ourselves and what our lives really mean.

We should treasure our life and what has been handed to us. You might say, "But you don't know my life. I have been through hell and back." Or, "My life has been so hard and it is not worth it." I am here to say your life matters and ALL Lives MATTER. Who you are in this life matters and it is a treasure to GOD. When you can feel it inside and know it inside that you are worth so much more than you realize then you can love anyone. I am not saying it will be easy at all. I have had people in my life that I just wanted to push away and say, "Well they have hurt me I don't have to love them." Saying that leaves an emptiness in my heart. If we are here to be like Jesus and show his unconditional love to everyone, then it should not matter what other people do or how they respond. Just show, give and receive LOVE.

With that being said it does not mean you let people walk all over you. It does not mean you let people hurt you or destroy you or the people around you. It means that loving others is a risk.

Measure is an amount or degree of something.

It can also mean an estimate of what is expected (as a person or situation).

How can we measure our lives? How can we measure our love for someone? Why measure love?

Treasure is something valuable that is hidden or kept in a safe place. It is something that is very special, important or valuable.

If you put these two words together and see there meaning, what does it make you feel inside?

If we live our lives by what is measured or given to us then we have missed the mark. If we can't see that our everyday life is a treasure then we have missed the mark.

We have to LOVE BEYOND measures. Meaning go past the finish line and keep going until your last breath. Love beyond the normal. Our lives belong to God so it is a treasure.

I have realized in my life that I want to stand for something, something bigger than myself. I want to love more than just what is expected of me. My life has taken different turns than what I expected it to take. People have come into my life that I would not have expected. People's stories have changed my thoughts and how I view life. When you get outside of your ideas and thoughts and into others, it allows your heart to have a deeper measure of how much you can really love people and see that their life is a treasure, just as much as your life is.

Give to someone you would not normally give to. I don't mean money because with money there is no emotional connection to the person or the situation. That person just might show you something about yourself.

Love beyond your walls. Love beyond your reach. Open your life up to feelings of love and forgiveness.

Treasure what is inside of you and know you were made in the image of God and there is no better image to be molded from. Also when you discover how important you are in this world and that you need love and want to give love, know that you are not alone in this discovery. People today just want to find hope and peace. We are only here for a short time so why not make the best of it and try our hardest to live a life filled with love, laughter, joy, peace and forgiveness.

LIVE LIKE IT MATTERS

AND

LOVE LIKE CRAZY

Live your life today for today, not tomorrow, and Love today for tomorrow.

Remember why you are here. What is your purpose on this earth? It is in loving other people when we grow the most and can learn to love ourselves even more. It takes the focus off ourselves and in loving others it gives us purpose. Live a life that is honest and loyal. Have integrity and conviction to where you let it shine because you are confident. Have meaning to your words, stand by your faith, and let your actions speak louder than your words, but let your words be with love and your actions be true.

Be CRAZY COURAGEOUS!!! Be bold and live your life everyday like it's your last. Leave no regret behind. Some people will try and push you down and tell you you're no good or all that love stuff is just a waste of time. Don't waste any time listening to them. Love when it's hard and leave the hate behind.

Let the evil and the judgment disappear and don't give it a second thought.

Let it make you stronger and overcome it. It might not seem possible to love certain people, but you can't give up, you have to keep trying.

Your family, your friends and even your enemies are counting on you because, if you don't,

WHO WILL?

Life is a treasure and it's not a pot of gold found on a ship or at the bottom of the ocean, but rather its value is worth more than any amount of gold.

Measure your treasure. Treasure your soul and treasure your heart.

Keep it close and be open to what is here and what is real.

LIVE with LOVE, LOVE your LIFE

Time will help you grow and time will show you where your life will go. Only experiences will lead you in the path of it all. Everything is right in front of you. Just open up and let yourself out and let people in.

Love without limits and Live without fear.

Take this challenge today and change your life. Take this declaration, this vow and make a change, a movement, and a promise to. . .

Live Like It Matters

And

Love Like Crazy!

LIVE LIKE IT MATTERS AND LOVE LIKE CRAZY

I vow to LIVE my life with purpose and truth.

I vow to not merely LIVE my life for myself but for others.

I vow to LIVE with honesty and be loyal in everything I do.

I vow to LIVE with integrity and conviction.

I vow to LIVE my life to the fullest and have meaning to my words and truth to my actions.

I vow to LIVE my life with strength and to be crazy courageous every day I am alive.

I vow to let LOVE lead me and leave the hate behind.

I vow to LOVE above evil and judgment.

I vow to LOVE when it just does not seem possible to LOVE.

I vow to LOVE my family, my friends and my enemies.

I vow to LOVE beyond measure because life is a treasure.

From this day forward, I vow to:

LIVE LIKE IT MATTERS AND LOVE LIKE CRAZY.

Sign _____ Date _____

For a copy of the Vows contact Beth Ann Stockton at llm479@yahoo.com

You receive a bracelet with the book.

Index

Page 22 Genesis 1:26-27 NIV

Page 24 Jeremiah 29:11 NIV

Page 25 Ephesians 6:14-18

Page 41 Proverbs 11:25

Page 49 Matthew 7:12

Page 54 Job 1:3

Page 55 Job 1:8-12, Job 2:7-10

Page 56 Job 1:21

Page 83 Daniel 1:3-7

Page 85 Daniel 2:27-28, Daniel 2:47-49

Page 86 Daniel 3:17-18

Page 88 Daniel 6:3-9

Page 89 Daniel 6:11, Daniel 6:16, Daniel 6:18-19

Page 93 Philippians 4:13

Index

Page 115 John 13:34

Page 116 1 John 4:16

Page 119 Luke 6:31

Page 123 1 John 4:8

Page 123 Corinthians 13:7-13

Page 124 Luke 6:41

Page 126 John 9:1-12

Page 127 John 9:13-16, John 9:18-25

Page 128 9:35-39

Page 130 Romans 12:9-20

Page 132 Luke 6:27-28

Page 135 Corinthians 13:4-8

Page 145 Proverbs 18:24

Page 147 Joshua 1:9

CHECK OUT MY WEBSITE

livelikeitmattersandlovelikecrazy.com

Coming soon

Live Like It Matters and Love Like Crazy

Youth, age 6-12

Vows based on the ages of 6-12 year olds and the struggles they deal with on a daily basis.

Live Like It Matters and Love Like Crazy

Teens, age 13-18.

Vows in this book, deal with the challenges that teens face.

For extra copies of the Vows or more bracelets please contact me at 623-695-6843 or e-mail me at llm479@yahoo.com

For public events, please feel free to contact me. Also, I would be honored to come to your school or church.

Thank you,

Beth Ann Stockton

Live Like It Matters

And

Love Like Crazy

By

Beth Ann Stockton

Copyright 2016 ©

Made in the USA
Columbia, SC
25 July 2023